General editor: Graham Handley MA Ph.D.

Brodie's Notes on Harper Lee's

To Kill a Mockingbird

Kenneth Hardacre MA
Formerly Head of English, Queens' School, Bushey, Hertfordshire

palgrave
macmillan

First published by James Brodie Ltd
First published 1976 by Pan Books Ltd
This revised edition published 1990

Published by
PALGRAVE MACMILLAN
Houndmills, Basingstoke, Hampshire RG21 6XS and
175 Fifth Avenue, New York, N.Y. 10010
Companies and representatives throughout the world

PALGRAVE MACMILLAN is the global academic imprint of the Palgrave
Macmillan division of St. Martin's Press, LLC and of Palgrave Macmillan Ltd.
Macmillan® is a registered trademark in the United States, United Kingdom
and other countries. Palgrave is a registered trademark in the European
Union and other countries.

ISBN 0–333– 58144-X

This book is printed on paper suitable for recycling and
made from fully managed and sustained forest sources.

Printed and bound in Great Britain by
Biddles Ltd., King's Lynn, Norfolk

ENL (LC) EE
R 64614 W

Contents

Preface

The intention throughout this study aid is to stimulate and guide, to encourage your involvement in the book, and to develop informed responses and a sure understanding of the main details.

Brodie's Notes provide a clear outline of the play or novel's plot, followed by act, scene, or chapter summaries and/or commentaries. These are designed to emphasize the most important literary and factual details. Poems, stories or non-fiction texts combine brief summary with critical commentary on individual aspects or common features of the genre being examined. Textual notes define what is difficult or obscure and emphasize literary qualities. Revision questions are set at appropriate points to test your ability to appreciate the prescribed book and to write accurately and relevantly about it.

In addition, each of these Notes includes a critical appreciation of the author's art. This covers such major elements as characterization, style, structure, setting and themes. Poems are examined technically – rhyme, rhythm, for instance. In fact, any important aspect of the prescribed work will be evaluated. The aim is to send you back to the text you are studying.

Each study aid concludes with a series of general questions which require a detailed knowledge of the book: some of these questions may invite comparison with other books, some will be suitable for coursework exercises, and some could be adapted to work you are doing on another book or books. Each study aid has been adapted to meet the needs of the current examination requirements. They provide a basic, individual and imaginative response to the work being studied, and it is hoped that they will stimulate you to acquire disciplined reading habits and critical fluency.

Graham Handley 1990

The author and her work

Many readers of *To Kill a Mockingbird* are surprised when they learn that Harper Lee is the professional name of a woman; yet this novel of events, seen through the eyes of a growing girl, clearly exemplifies qualities of intuition, personal understanding and warm sympathy. It is perhaps less surprising that its author should have been a law student: the novel emphasizes the importance of law in the community and demonstrates a detailed knowledge of its workings.

Born in 1926, Nelle Harper Lee was the youngest daughter of Amasa Coleman Lee and Frances Lee. Her father Amasa was a lawyer and practised in Monroeville, Alabama which is almost certainly the 'Maycomb' of her novel. Harper Lee began writing at the age of seven and, like Jem and Scout in her story, she attended the local schools. She appears to have formed some shrewd and critical opinions about education – a subject on which both Scout and Atticus have some searching comments to make. After a short period at Huntington College, Miss Lee attended the State University of Alabama at Tuscaloosa where she read law. This stay at university was broken by a year spent as an exchange student at Oxford University. In 1950, she left Alabama for New York, six months prior to her final law exams. In retrospect, Harper Lee felt that her years in law school were 'good training for a writer'.

In New York, Harper Lee worked as an airline reservations clerk until, encouraged by an agent who had seen her work and by friends who offered financial support, she gave up her job and devoted her energies to full-time writing. The manuscript of *To Kill a Mockingbird* was first submitted to a publisher in 1957 and after much re-writing was published two-and-a-half years later.

To Kill a Mockingbird was an astonishing first novel. It was published in 1960, and in the following year won three awards: the Pulitzer Prize, the Alabama Literary Association Award and the Brotherhood Award of the National Conference of Christians and Jews. It also won the Bestsellers' paperback of the year award for 1962. It has sold millions of copies and has been translated into many languages. In 1962, from a screenplay adaptation by Horton Foote, Universal-International Pictures made a film of *To Kill a Mockingbird*, in which the parts of Scout and Atticus were played by Mary Badham and Gregory Peck respectively.

No second novel has appeared but one is promised. It too will centre on southern small-town life, described by Miss Lee as 'the last refuge of eccentrics'. As a writer, Harper Lee believes her chief literary debt is to Jane Austen, 'writing, cameo-like in that little corner of the world of hers and making it universal'.

Setting and plot

Setting

The setting for the story is Maycomb, 'a tired old town' in Alabama, 'an island in a patchwork sea of cotton fields and timber land'. 'Its buildings are solid,' we are told, 'its court-house proud, its streets graciously wide.' We learn of its main square, with its live oak trees and giant monkey-puzzle bushes and its public hitching rail. Here, among square-faced stores and steep-roofed houses, is the county court-house, a strange architectural medley of Greek columns, Victorian vistas and a big 19th-century clock tower. This building housed the offices of many of the county officials and Atticus himself, until he moved to the quieter quarters of the nearby Maycomb Bank building. Not far away is the Maycomb jail, 'a miniature Gothic joke, one cell wide and two cells high, complete with tiny battlements and flying buttresses' and wedged between Tyndal's Hardware Store and the office of the *Maycomb Tribune*. Surrounding the court-house square is a larger square of stores, like V. J. Elmore's and the Mayco Drugstore and here too, no doubt, is the Jitney Jungle.

The Finches live on the main residential street in town, where the inhabitants are accustomed to sit on their front porches in summer and where 'closed doors meant illness and cold weather only'. Outside the southern town limits, across the old sawmill tracks, are the Quarters, the district where the Blacks live in their neat, snug cabins (very different from the squalid mess of the Ewells' cabin behind the town garbage dump) and worship in their church, the only one in Maycomb with a steeple and bell.

The professional families of Maycomb form a small and intimate community, where life is lived informally. The local telephone operator, Miss Eula May, knows everyone's voice and is 'entrusted with issuing public announcements, wedding invitations, setting off the fire siren, and giving first-aid instructions when Dr Reynolds was away'. Not surprisingly, everyone's business is quickly known – a situation in which gossips like Miss Stephanie Crawford thrive.

Life in Maycomb is for the most part quiet and unhurried.

People take their time about everything. Sunday visiting and Missionary Circle tea parties are high on the list of activities of Maycomb's professional families. The settled 'caste system' of these families is rarely disturbed by new people settling in Maycomb and life maintains a very even tenor. 'In Maycomb grown men stood outside in the front yard for only two reasons: death and politics.' *To Kill a Mockingbird* tells of much that happens to disturb that even tenor. As Atticus humorously says, 'From rape to riot to runaways. I wonder what the next two hours will bring.'

In Chapter 13 there is a sketch of Maycomb's early growth and history, and legacies of the past still remain in men's minds and attitudes. There are many references to events and persons connected with the American Civil War (Alabama was one of the slave states which formed themselves into the Southern Confederation) and many of the prejudices aroused then still remain (see, for example, the unfortunate way in which Miss Caroline Fisher introduces herself to her first class in Chapter 2). We also learn of some of the fundamentalist religious sects, like Mennonites and foot-washing Baptists, which flourish in the southern states. Above all, throughout the book, one is aware of the anti-Black feeling of the southern states, at a time when Ku Klux Klan activity was still remembered (see note on 'Ku Klux Klan', p.40).

The period of the story of *To Kill a Mockingbird*, some thirty years before the growth of the Civil Rights movement, is the time of the New Deal, the name given to the social and economic policies introduced by President Franklin D. Roosevelt in 1933 to meet the acute depression which had begun in 1929 after a widespread series of bank failures. Maycomb County was farming country and the economic crash hit farmers hardest. As Scout tells us at the beginning of her story:

There was no hurry, for there was nowhere to go, nothing to buy and no money to buy it with, nothing to see outside the boundaries of Maycomb County. But it was a time of vague optimism for some of the people: Maycomb County had recently been told that it had nothing to fear but fear itself. (Chapter 1, p.11)

Plot

To Kill a Mockingbird is the story of 'growing up' – in understanding and sympathy as well as in age; a development in depth as well as in time; a growth of awareness which affects others besides the two children who are at the heart of the story. Indeed, it throws an important light over an area of human experience wider than the small town that provides the story's setting. The process of expansion in sympathy and understanding, the increasing awareness, is also experienced by the reader, who 'grows' in the course of reading a novel which shows us that fear and hatred spring from ignorance and lack of understanding.

The novel recalls the events of two years or so, from summer 1933 to Halloween 1935, as seen through the eyes of Scout (Jean Louise) and Jem, the children of Atticus Finch, who is a lawyer in Maycomb, a small town in the southern state of Alabama. Their lives are at first mainly concerned with school and home, their games and their reading. They enjoy a growing relationship with all their neighbours except the Radleys. This family has cut itself off from the rest of Maycomb on account of what the children believe to be mysterious crimes committed long ago by their younger son. Although they nickname him Boo Radley, Jem and Scout regard him with terror as a 'malevolent phantom' with evil powers. Their friend Dill, who visits them in the summer holidays each year, invents the new game of 'making Boo Radley come out' and they play several variations on this. Slowly their initial impression of Boo Radley changes as first Jem and then Scout come to realize that his intentions are friendly.

They find that life changes for them in many ways when their father undertakes the defence of a Black charged with the rape of a white girl. They now face opposition from the townsfolk and begin to experience the force of prejudice. Though Atticus fails to overcome the prejudice of the jury, and the defendant, though innocent, is found guilty, the victim's father threatens all those connected with the case. His threats find their expression in the climax of the novel when he attacks Scout and Jem as they are returning in the darkness from a Halloween pageant. Their lives are saved by a strange and gentle person – Boo Radley, who (Scott later realizes) has watched over the Finch children during these last two years with interest and affection.

Themes

To Kill a Mockingbird is a story that has many themes. Primarily, of course, it is, as we have said, a story about growing up and it shows how two children come to have a deeper understanding of the world and the people around them. The circumstances and events through which they live during the two years or so with which the novel deals are wide enough to throw light for them on many aspects of life.

In this novel Harper Lee touches on many social questions. Foremost among these is the *colour problem* in the southern states of America in the mid 1930s. The focus for this is the charge brought by Bob Ewell against Tom Robinson and the way in which the anti-Black feeling in Maycomb is the cause of animosity towards Atticus and his family because of his defence of Tom. It is manifested in the Cunninghams' attempt to lynch Tom and Mr Gilmer's contemptuous cross-examination in the courtroom. It is also evident in Aunt Alexandra's disapproval of Calpurnia and in the hypocritical attitudes of Miss Gates and the ladies of the Missionary Circle.

The 'rigid and time-honoured code' of society was that, while white people could employ and even exploit Blacks, there could be no personal relationship between Black and White and no recognition that Blacks had the same reactions and feelings as white people. Further, there was an evil assumption 'that *all* Blacks lie, that *all* Blacks are basically immoral beings'. They certainly did not have the benefit of the supposed impartiality of the law. The Reverend Sykes says, 'I ain't ever seen any jury decide in favour of a coloured man over a white man.' Atticus does not understand 'why reasonable people go stark raving mad when anything involving a Negro comes up' and he calls this emotional attitude 'Maycomb's usual disease'. Mr Dolphus Raymond talks about 'the hell white people give coloured folks, without even stopping to think that they're people, too'. Atticus fears that 'one of these days we're going to pay the bill for it'.

The *bigotry* of some fundamentalist religious sects is touched on in the introduction of the foot-washing Baptists who criticize Miss Maudie Atkinson. Her conversation with Scout on this subject leads Scout to think about what is implied by a good and a reasonable life.

Scout also ponders over the lip-service paid to the ideal of democracy ('equal rights for all, special privileges for none') when contrasted with the realities of intolerance and prejudice: for example, the horror expressed by Miss Gates at Hitler's persecution of the Jews and her own intolerance of Blacks. This is one of many instances in the novel of the contrast between reason (represented by the character of Atticus) and prejudice, which is born of ignorance and fear. At different points in the story we find many characters who are misunderstood through ignorance and fear: Tom Robinson, Mayella Ewell, the Cunninghams, Mr Dolphus Raymond, Boo Radley. One of the reasons why Jem and Scout are so free from prejudice is that they have been brought up by a lawyer and a Black.

Much is said about *education*. Miss Harper Lee gives Scout a very critical view of methods of teaching and of some educational jargon in Chapters 2, 3 and 4, and Atticus voices his criticism of some educational philosophies in his speech to the jury in Chapter 20. Certainly Scout learns more from Atticus and Calpurnia and from her experiences outside school than from her formal schooling.

The novel presents material for an interesting study of various kinds of relationship between parents and children. Dill's parents are simply not interested in him. Aunt Alexandra's son 'left home as soon as was humanly possible'. He and his wife deposit *their* son with his grandparents every Christmas in order to pursue their own pleasures. Mayella Ewell suffers from neglect and cruelty from her father. The Radleys' shame and excessive anxiety stifle and suffocate the personality of their younger son, Arthur. Jem and Scout, on the other hand, are brought up with tolerance, reason, a sense of compassion, a set of values.

Loneliness is also described through many of the characters in this novel. Boo Radley, Tom Robinson and Mayella Ewell are all outcasts, isolated and rejected. Mr Dolphus Raymond has accepted his rejection and turned it to his advantage. Boo Radley and Tom Robinson are 'mockingbird' figures (see p.15/16) who are needlessly tormented by society. Mayella lacks love and understanding, and her need for these brings about Tom's downfall. Scout comes to see her as the loneliest person in the world. 'She was even lonelier than Boo Radley, who had not been out of the house in twenty-five years.'

Many facets of *courage* are shown in *To Kill a Mockingbird*: the physical courage of Atticus facing the Cunningham gang and the mad dog; the spiritual courage of Mrs Dubose, determined to break her addiction to morphine before she dies; the cheerfulness with which Miss Maudie Atkinson accepts the loss of her house through fire; the courage which is required to carry through one's mundane job in the face of antipathy and opposition – as Atticus does in taking on the defence of Tom Robinson. Courage involves things like fighting with your head rather than with your fists and living with your own conscience. 'It's when you know you're licked before you begin,' says Atticus, 'but you begin anyway and you see it through no matter what.'

Much of *To Kill a Mockingbird* is concerned with what the poet Robert Burns called *man's inhumanity to man* and what Mr Dolphus Raymond calls 'the simple hell people give other people'. We witness Bob Ewell's inhumanity towards his daughter; the inhumanity shown by the Radleys towards their son; the inhumanity shown by white people towards Blacks. On another level we see how artificial barriers between people are created by vague conceptions like 'breeding' and 'background' and 'our kind of folks'. The children find all this difficult to understand. Jem has a theory that 'there's four kinds of folks in the world' (Chapter 23), but Scout thinks there is just one kind of folks. But if there is, asks Jem, why can't they get along with each other? 'If they're all alike, why do they go out of their way to despise each other?' Understanding adults and their world *is* difficult. Scout is often confused and rebellious; Dill is at first disillusioned and then cynical; Jem finds it a sad business and at one point he thinks he understands why Boo Radley never comes out of the house: 'it's because he *wants* to stay inside'.

The most important lesson they learn comes from Atticus, the lesson of *compassion*.

'First of all,' he said, 'if you can learn a simple trick, Scout, you'll get along a lot better with all kinds of folks. You never really understand a person until you consider things from his point of view –'
  'Sir?'
  '– until you climb into his skin and walk around in it.' (Chapter 3, p.35)

In the course of the novel Scout 'climbs into the skin' of Miss Fisher, Walter Cunningham, Jem, Mrs Dubose and Boo Radley. She also learns to respect the *differences* between people, as Calpurnia and Mr Dolphus Raymond have learned to do.

To Kill a Mockingbird ultimately leaves us with cause for hope. The trial and death of Tom Robinson is a sickening business, but the jury does take a long time to reach its verdict and this is regarded as significant by both Miss Maudie ('We're making a step – it's just a baby-step, but it's a step') and Atticus ('This may be the shadow of a beginning'). Scout and Jem learn that most people are 'real nice' when you finally see them. They begin to understand adults and the adult world of which they will soon be part – thanks to people like Atticus and Miss Maudie.

The mockingbird symbolism

Initially, the title of this book is merely a cryptic phrase; ultimately the reader sees it as part of an important piece of symbolism – that is, part of a process by which an object represents something more important than itself, is associated with a wider significance and eventually takes on the power of profound imaginative suggestion.

The symbol of the mockingbird, with its associated ideas, appears at several points in the novel. It first occurs in Chapter 10, where Atticus says the children may shoot all the bluejays they want 'but remember it's a sin to kill a mockingbird'. This is the first time Scout has ever heard him say it was a sin to do something. The full significance of this remark is explained to Scout by Miss Maudie Atkinson. Mockingbirds do not 'eat up people's gardens' or 'nest in corncribs'; they do nothing but 'sing their hearts out for us', making music for us to enjoy. They represent a type of gentle, harmless creature, innocent and beautiful. To kill a mockingbird would be wicked and spiteful, a senseless and pointless act of destruction.

Destruction is wholly alien to Atticus's way of life. He is an unusually skilful marksman but he regards this gift as one that gives him 'an unfair advantage over most living things' and he has therefore given up hunting. But there are occasions when he has to shoot and the appearance in the street of the mad dog is one of them. As Atticus prepares to shoot the dog, everything goes quiet. 'The trees were still, the mockingbirds were silent, the carpenters at Miss Maudie's house had vanished.' The dog is killed in front of the Radley Place.

These circumstances add depth and intensity to the next occasion when mockingbirds are mentioned, in Chapter 21. The courtroom awaits the return of the jury with their verdict and Scout experiences the same feeling as on that February morning, 'when the mockingbirds were still, and the carpenters had stopped hammering . . . and every wood door in the neighbourhood was shut as tight as the doors of the Radley Place'. It was, she says, like watching Atticus walk into the street, raise his rifle to his shoulder and pull the trigger – 'but watching all the time knowing that the gun was empty'. The verdict of guilty is a sad blow – though Atticus knew that on this occasion he was 'licked' before he began – a wicked and senseless act of persecution. Tom Robinson, a gentle and harmless creature, who felt sorry for Mayella Ewell and wished to help her, has become a mockingbird figure. Later, his death (he is shot in a desperate attempt to escape) is represented to us as another act of pointless destruction. Mr Underwood explains this in his editorial:

> Mr Underwood simply figured it was a sin to kill cripples, be they standing, sitting, or escaping. He likened Tom's death to the senseless slaughter of songbirds by hunters and children. (Chapter 25, p.245)

Scout comes to realize that Boo Radley is another mockingbird type – one who does no harm but who has been persecuted in some way, by gossip and by society's attitude, and by the children's actions. Boo Radley and the mockingbird are first linked when Jem and Scout start on their 'longest journey together', on their way to the Halloween pageant. As they pass the Radley Place

> Jem said, 'Boo must not be at home. Listen.'
> High above us in the darkness a solitary mocker poured out his repertoire in blissful unawareness of whose tree he sat in. (Chapter 28, p.259)

Towards the end of the story, Heck Tate says to Atticus that it would be wrong to do anything but leave Boo Radley alone, 'draggin' him with his shy ways into the limelight – to me, that's a sin'. And Scout adds: 'Well, it'd be sort of like shootin' a mockingbird, wouldn't it?'

In this way the mockingbird image brings together two of the main characters in the book, Tom Robinson and Boo Radley.

Structure and style

Structure

The structure of the novel has a pleasing symmetry. At the centre of Part 1 is the children's fear of Boo Radley; at the centre of Part 2 is Bob Ewell's hatred of Tom Robinson. Later, this hatred is directed towards Atticus's children and their lives are saved by Boo Radley, the former object of their fear: thus the plot of Part 2 is neatly joined to that of Part 1. In the section devoted almost exclusively to Tom Robinson and Bob Ewell, the thread of Part 1 is kept in the reader's mind by references to Boo Radley (Chapters 15, 19, 23 and 26).

Part 1 may be subdivided into two sections:

Chapters 1–8: Boo Radley
1 Home
2–3 School
4–8 'Making Boo Radley come out'

Chapters 9–11: Gathering Shadows
Opposition, first from children (Cecil Jacobs and cousin Francis) and later from adults (Mrs Dubose).

Part 2 may be subdivided into four sections:

Chapters 12–15: Prelude to the trial
16–21 The trial of Tom Robinson
22–28 Aftermath: Ewell's attack
29–31 Boo Radley again.

Each of these sections works up to its own dramatic climax – in Chapter 8 the burning of Miss Maudie's house and the unnoticed appearance of Boo Radley; in Chapter 11 the episode of Mrs Dubose; in Chapter 15 the 'attack' on Maycomb jail; in Chapter 21 the end of the trial; in Chapter 28 Ewell's attack on the children and his death; in Chapter 31 Scout's recognition of Boo Radley's love and protection.

There is another interesting contrast between Part 1 and Part 2. Part 1 is largely concerned with the way the children come to understand more about people as individuals – at school, young

Walter Cunningham and Miss Caroline Fisher; at home, Miss Maudie Atkinson, Mrs Dubose and, of course, Boo Radley. In Part 2, on the other hand, the emphasis is on the wider social situation. First, Aunt Alexandra's arrival and her views on propriety and the bringing up of children lead them to think about the family as a social unit. Soon they become aware of the prejudices and injustices in the community as a whole. These have their focal point in the trial of Tom Robinson and they are also revealed in the contrast between Miss Gates's Current Events lesson and her comment on Tom Robinson's conviction, and in the opinions of the Missionary Circle. Part 2 also emphasizes the divisions in society (Mr Dolphus Raymond, the Ewells, the sad plight of 'mixed' children, in Chapter 16, and the visit to Calpurnia's church are important here) and the children's own attempts to understand the view of the adults on family pride, 'gentle breeding', background and 'fine folks'. 'If there's just one kind of folks, why can't they get along with each other? If they're all alike, why do they go out of their way to despise each other?'

Over the basic plan, as outlined above, are laid many details which lend strength and interest to the structure of the novel. The character of Miss Maudie Atkinson, though not involved in the plot, is of great importance in every section of the novel in helping the children to understand the significance of their experiences. The Cunningham family are subtly used to provide a thread which links many sections of the story.

Throughout the book there are effective echoes and contrasts. At the end of the first chapter Jem touches Boo's house in fear and daring; at the end of the last chapter Boo touches the sleeping Jem with love and affection. The wider lessons of school and the opinions of Miss Gates in Chapter 26 recall the wider lessons and the opinions of Miss Fisher in Chapters 2 and 3. In Chapter 9, Scout is so enraged by taunts against Atticus that she attacks her cousin and, thanks to Atticus, learns much from the episode; in Chapter 11, Jem is so enraged by Mrs Dubose's charges against Atticus that he attacks her camellias and, thanks to Atticus, he too learns much. The growth of insight and understanding in Jem, from his discussions with Atticus about the verdict at the Robinson trial in Chapter 23, is paralleled by the growth of insight and understanding in Scout, from Miss Maudie's part in the Missionary Circle tea-party in Chapter 24.

There are significant repetitions and echoes of phrase which lend a unity to the story – like Miss Maudie's phrase about Atticus being the same in his house (and in the courtroom) as he is on the public streets (see Chapters 5 and 19), a phrase which Atticus himself echoes in his discussion with the sheriff in Chapter 30. Parallel with phrases like this are the repetitions of small personal gestures at significant moments in the story, like Atticus's pushing up his glasses to his forehead, which in Scout's mind links the anxieties over Tom Robinson (Chapter 16) with the shooting of the mad dog (Chapter 10) and combines with a recollection of another of Atticus's gestures – calmly folding his newspaper and pushing back his hat (Chapters 15 and 16). Again the silent apprehension as the jury files in to give its verdict (Chapter 21) recalls for Scout an earlier episode:

The feeling grew until the atmosphere in the court-room was exactly the same as a cold February morning, when the mockingbirds were still, and the carpenters had stopped hammering on Miss Maudie's new house, and every wood door in the neighbourhood was shut as tight as the doors of the Radley Place. A deserted, waiting, empty street, and the court-room was packed with people. A steaming summer night was no different from a winter morning . . . I expected Mr Tate to say any minute, 'Take him, Mr Finch . . .' (Chapter 21, p.214).

This passage is connected with the imaginative use of the mockingbird symbolism (see p.14).

Another effective structural device is used almost at the end of the novel when Scout, having accompanied Arthur Radley back to his house, stands before the shuttered window and imagines the events of the last two years as they would have appeared to Boo Radley, watching from inside that same window.

Narrative method

The story of *To Kill a Mockingbird* is presented to us as a series of events observed by a young girl. Admittedly Scout is a precocious child (at the beginning of the story she is not quite six years old). Behind the young girl, of course, is the adult that she grew into – for we are led to understand that the novel is the story as recalled by an older Scout looking back at her childhood. 'When enough years had gone by to enable us to look back on them, we sometimes discussed the events leading to his (Jem's) accident' (Chapter 1, p.9). And behind this again is the literary experience of Miss Harper Lee – her knowledge of people and things, her literary skills and style, her vocabulary.

Nevertheless, we are given the impression that the events unfold as they appeared to the young Scout; and this narrative method has considerable effectiveness as a result of Scout's youth and innocence.

First, it is a source of humour, as (for example) when Scout innocently reports Miss Maudie's question to Miss Stephanie Crawford ('What did you do, Stephanie, move over in bed . . .?') without understanding the sexual innuendo behind it (Chapter 5, p.51), or in the way Scout picks up and uses the term 'morphodite' without understanding the hermaphrodite qualities of Jem's snowman.

Secondly, some of the ugliness and horror of a series of events which include a charge of rape, the senseless sacrifice of Tom Robinson, the attack on two children by Bob Ewell and his death at the hands of Boo Radley, can be toned down by being presented in this way.

Thirdly, the reader gains an additional interest by his ability to perceive significance where Scout is not aware of it. She does not at first see the significance of the gifts in the knot-hole; she does not understand the full implications of a charge of rape or the full horror of Mayella Ewell's actions, and when Scout overhears and reports Atticus's remarks about this she does so without knowing exactly what he means.

Fourthly, because of the above aspect, Miss Lee is able to contrast effectively Scout's ingenuousness, the justice, rationality and straightforwardness of children and, on the other hand, the hypocrisy, prejudice, the perversion of justice and the sordid adult values which are implicit in many of the events she relates. Both Atticus ('So far nothing in your life has interfered with your reasoning process') and Mr Dolphus Raymond ('Because you're children and you can understand it') comment on the children's advantage.

The student should also note how, in Chapter 25, Miss Lee overcomes the problem of relating events at which our narrator was not present.

Style

Miss Harper Lee's language is straightforward and varied. The realistic and exact dialogue is full of colloquialisms from the southern states of America. The descriptive passages are notable for their detailed observation and precise expression. Consider this description of Walter Cunningham:

Walter looked as if he had been raised on fish food: his eyes, as blue as Dill Harris's, were redrimmed and watery. There was no colour in his face except at the tip of his nose, which was moistly pink. He fingered the straps of his overalls, nervously picking at the metal hooks. (Chapter 3, p.29)

or the paragraph (beginning 'Something had happened to her') which describes Mrs Dubose's face in Chapter 11, p.113.

The variety of the writing ranges from clean-cut logic and the dramatic cut-and-thrust of Atticus's cross-examination in the courtroom to the mystery and suspense which are found in the description of the Radley Place (Chapter 1), the account of the children's visit there one night (Chapter 6) and the attack which is made upon them on Halloween and their rescue by a mysterious stranger (Chapter 28). Miss Lee can convey a feeling of unreality in a passage like this:

What happened after that had a dreamlike quality: in a dream I saw the jury return, moving like underwater swimmers, and Judge Taylor's voice came from far away, and was tiny. I saw something only a lawyer's child could be expected to see, could be expected to watch for, and it was like watching Atticus walk into the street, raise a rifle to his shoulder and pull the trigger, but watching all the time knowing that the gun was empty. (Chapter 21, p.215)

At other times she can clothe an abstraction in a series of sense impressions:

Summer was our best season: it was sleeping on the back screened porch in cots, or trying to sleep in the tree-house; summer was everything good to eat; it was a thousand colours in a parched landscape; but most of all, summer was Dill. (Chapter 4, p.40)

or through a string of events:

Somehow it was hotter then: a black dog suffered on a summer's day; bony mules hitched to Hoover carts flicked flies in the sweltering shade of the live oaks on the square. Men's stiff collars wilted by nine in the morning. Ladies bathed before noon, after their three o'clock naps, and by nightfall were like soft tea-cakes with frostings of sweat and sweet talcum. (Chapter 1, p.11)

Accurate observation and liveliness of expression are often evident in thumb-nail sketches of minor characters, like those of

Mr Gilmer (Chapter 17) and Mrs Gertrude Farrow (Chapter 24); and Miss Lee's writing constantly pleases by the use of striking phrases. The shadow of a man, moving across the Radley porch, is 'crisp as toast' (Chapter 6); Mayella Ewell gains a kind of stealthy confidence, 'like a steady-eyed cat with a twitchy tail' (Chapter 18); Scout refers to her father's 'last-will-and-testament diction' (Chapter 3).

The use of simile and metaphor is particularly effective. The ground around the cabin of the Ewells looks 'like the playhouse of an insane child'; if Miss Maudie found a blade of nut-grass in her garden, it was 'like the Second Battle of the Marne'; Miss Stephanie Crawford is described as 'that English Channel of gossip'. When Scout overheard a conversation that suggested that her aunt had plans for bringing her up more strictly, she 'felt the starched walls of a pink cotton penitentiary' closing in on her. Sometimes it is a single word that is effective: when Scout is rolled inside the tyre, 'Ground, sky and houses melted into a mad *palette*'.

At the other end of the scale there are many extended passages of description and discussion which demonstrate the versatility and suppleness of Miss Lee's handling of language. Examples are: the discussion of education at the beginning of Chapter 4; the account of the growth of Maycomb in Chapter 13; the description of Maycomb jail in Chapter 15; and the story of Colonel Maycomb in Chapter 28. The gently ironic humour of these passages is characteristic of the novel as a whole and an important element in a story which is so often critical of human behaviour.

Chapter summaries, textual notes and revision questions

Part 1
Chapter 1

The narrator of the story, Jean Louise Finch (known as Scout), and her brother Jem are the children of Atticus Finch, a lawyer of Maycomb in the state of Alabama. Their mother had died when Jem and Scout were six and two years old respectively. The children discuss the accident in which Jem, who was almost thirteen at the time, badly broke his arm. Scout suggests that the Ewells started it all; but Jem thinks it all started during the summer of 1933, when Dill (Charles Baker Harris) first stayed with his aunt, Miss Rachel Haverford. Dill was nearly seven, Scout almost six and Jem nearly ten.

In the 'tired old town' of Maycomb, with its unhurried pace of life, the Finch household (Atticus, Jem, Scout and Calpurnia, the Black cook) live in the main residential street. The neighbouring houses are occupied by Miss Haverford, Mrs Dubose, Miss Stephanie Crawford, Miss Maudie Atkinson and the Radleys.

The Radley home is regarded with mystery and fear by the children. The family had cut itself off from their neighbours twenty years previously, when their younger boy, Arthur, fell into bad ways and ran into trouble with the police. Many stories had grown up around Arthur, now thirty-eight years old and nicknamed Boo Radley by the children; because he is never seen they regard him as a 'malevolent phantom'. The house holds a sinister fascination for them and Dill invents the game of 'making Boo Radley come out', daring Jem to go up to the Radley house.

Lawyers ... children once (epigraph). From 'Old Benchers of the Inner Temple' in *Essays of Elia* by Charles Lamb (1775–1834), essayist, poet and prolific letter-writer.
Andrew Jackson Lawyer and soldier (1767–1845), who became the seventh President of the United States (1829–37). In 1813, as major-general of the Tennessee militia, Jackson defeated the Creeks, a confederacy of Indian tribes which had been devastating Georgia and Alabama.

Alabama The main river of the state of Alabama. It joins the Tombigbee and flows into the Gulf of Mexico at Mobile.

Atticus The original bearer of the name was a Roman, Titus Pomponius (109–32 BC). During the civil war he fled to Athens and became so much a part of Greek life and literature that he was given the name Atticus (from the Greek state Attica – Athens was its capital). He resolved never to become involved in politics; he sided with neither faction in the civil war; Caesar and Pompey, Brutus and Antony were among his friends. In the light of this, note the significance of Atticus Finch's initial appearance in this novel and of the way he settles his children's difference of opinion.

Mobile The chief port of Alabama, on the Gulf of Mexico. Note how a novel which deals in part with the persecution of Blacks starts with Simon Finch's emigration to escape from the persecution of Methodists in England in the second half of the eighteenth century.

John Wesley The founder of Wesleyan Methodism spent two years (1735–7) in Georgia, the neighbouring state to Alabama, preaching to the colonists.

disturbance...South i.e. the American Civil War. Alabama was one of the slave-holding states which seceded from the Union and in 1861 formed themselves into a Southern Confederation.

Montgomery County seat of Montgomery County and state capital of Alabama.

trot-lines Long lines with baited fish-hooks a few feet apart.

Maycomb A fictitious name. The way of life and some of the details of 'Maycomb' are almost certainly based on Monroeville, the author's home town. If 'Maycomb' is Monroeville, then 'Finch's Landing', 32 km (20 miles) to the west, would be somewhere in the neighbourhood of Jackson.

checker-board i.e. for draughts or chess.

Code of Alabama A large volume containing a summary of all the laws which pertained especially to the state of Alabama.

live oaks Live oak is the name of an American evergreen oak which grows in the southern Atlantic states.

Hoover carts A kind of mule cart, so named because of the then President Herbert Hoover.

dispatched i.e. murdered.

but fear itself In his first Inaugural Address as President of the United States on 4 March 1933, Franklin D. Roosevelt had said: 'Let me assert my firm belief that the only thing we have to fear is fear itself.'

collard A variety of cabbage or kale. The word is an American corruption of 'colewort'.

Shoot 'An exclamation expressing annoyance' (Webster).

Dracula A film based on the classic English horror story about vampires which was written in 1897 by Bram Stoker.

cowlick A tuft of turned-up hair on the forehead, so called because it looks as if it has been licked by a cow.

chinaberry trees American name for the azederac, a very tall tree, sometimes known as bead-tree.

Oliver Optic Pen name of William Taylor Adams (1822–97), a prolific writer of several series of stories for boys.

Victor Appleton Another author of popular boys' stories.

Edgar Rice Burroughs American novelist (1875–1950), author of more than a dozen very popular books about Tarzan, a boy who was adopted and brought up by apes. The first of these books, *Tarzan of the Apes*, was published in 1912.

The Rover Boys The heroes of a popular series of books for boys about life in a preparatory school. The first (of thirty!) appeared in 1899. They were written by Edward Stratemeyer (1862-1930), under the pen-name of Arthur M. Winfield.

Tom Swift A boy-inventor, hero of a long series of novels for boys written by Edward Stratemeyer.

Merlin An enchanter in the Arthurian romances. His magical powers served King Arthur well on several occasions.

picket i.e. a picket-fence, a fence of wooden stakes.

johnson grass A kind of tropical grass similar to Indian corn, sometimes grown for grain in the southern states of America. It is named after William Johnson, a 19th-century American agriculturalist.

rabbit-tobacco A kind of balsam weed, sometimes used for smoking.

pecan The North American hickory, a tree of the walnut family.

younger Radley boy i.e. Arthur, referred to by the children as Boo.

Cunninghams Note this first mention of a family whose members are to play an important part in the story. Old Sarum is a fictitious place name.

Abbotsville Almost certainly a fictitious name.

flivver Slang for a cheap car.

beadle A minor official with power to punish petty offenders.

probate judge Probate is usually concerned with wills and the estates of deceased persons. Perhaps here the word 'probate' implies putting young people on probation.

Auburn A town in Lee County about 200 km (125 miles) north-east of Monroeville.

Tuscaloosa Until 1846 Tuscaloosa was the state capital. It is the seat of the University of Alabama.

cannas The canna is the Indian shot, a genus of tropical plant with showy flowers and foliage.

Pensacola A city and port of Florida on the Gulf of Mexico not far from the state boundary with Alabama.

a reasonable description Jem's description owes more to local gossip and his reading of sensational literature than to reason or observation!

The Grey Ghost Presumably the title of a story for boys. The book is referred to again in the final pages of Chapter 31 as being written by 'Seckatary Hawkins'.

two Tom Swifts See note above.
yard American term for garden.

Chapter 2

In September Dill returns to Meridian and Scout starts school. The lessons of her teacher, Miss Caroline Fisher, are at first out of touch with the interests and outlook of her pupils. Surprised that Scout can already read, she says that Atticus is not to teach her any more. Miss Fisher fails to understand why Walter Cunningham has brought no lunch. The incident leads to Scout's recalling her knowledge of 'the Cunningham tribe' and of how Walter's father paid for Atticus's services with gifts of nuts and vegetables. Miss Fisher interprets Scout's rather precocious knowledge as impertinence and punishes her – ineffectually.

Tarzan and the Ant Men See note on 'Edgar Rice Burroughs' above.
in a daze Jem probably had a schoolboy crush on the young Miss Fisher.
Union See note on 'disturbance . . . South' above.
Big Mules Possibly a reference to the importance of the cotton industry; a mule is a cotton-spinning machine.
catawba An American grape, named after the river in South Carolina where it was found.
union suit Undergarment consisting of combined shirt and drawers.
Dewey Decimal System A system for the classification of books in libraries, named after its inventor, Melvil Dewey (1851–1931), an American librarian. It has been widely adopted throughout the world. Jem is confused, of course.
Molasses A thick treacle. The 'buckets' or tins used in the refining of raw sugar were now used by the children as lunch containers.
hookworms The disease caused by this parasite gives the sufferer an anaemic appearance.
Yeb'm i.e. yes, ma'am.
quarter A 25-cent piece (a quarter of a dollar).
on Walter's behalf Scout's intervention has important repercussions later in the novel (see Chapters 15 and 23).
scrip stamps Charity tokens which can be exchanged for goods.
entailment The settlement of land upon a person or persons other than the owner.
smilax A plant of the lily family, much used for decoration.
croker-sack A sack made of coarse material (e.g. burlap).
turnip greens In England, turnip-tops: the green sprouts of the turnip used as a vegetable.

crash The acute economic depression which had begun in 1929.
nickels Five-cent pieces.
dimes Silver coins worth ten cents.
WPA Works Progress Administration was one of the reforms
  introduced in the mid 1930s by President Franklin D. Roosevelt. It was
  a scheme to provide work relief for the unemployed, chiefly to enable
  them to maintain their skills and their self-respect.
whipped The word is used loosely for 'punished'.

Chapter 3

Jem stops Scout's fight with Walter Cunningham and invites him
to dinner. As they pass the Radley Place they talk of Boo Radley.
Though Walter's schooling has been neglected, over the meal he
can discuss farm problems with Atticus like an adult. After
Scout's comments on Walter's fondness for molasses with his
meat she is read a lecture by Calpurnia on the proper treatment
of guests. In class that afternoon Miss Fisher is horrified when
she sees a louse crawl out of the hair of one of her pupils, Burris
Ewell, and she learns something of the Ewells before Burris
leaves, hurling abuse at her. That evening, depressed because of
Miss Fisher's ban on reading at home, Scout does not wish to go
to school any more. Atticus discusses with her the real lessons of
school learned by both Scout and Miss Fisher that day; the
position of the Ewells (whose children went to school on the first
day only) in relation to the law, and the meaning of compromise.
Scout agrees to go to school and Atticus agrees that they will
continue to read together in the evenings.

haint Ghost. Southerners refer to a ghost as a 'haunt': 'haint' is a dialect
  form of this.
Miss Priss Name for a prim female.
field size i.e. old enough to work in the fields.
what the sam hill Sam Hill is probably a euphemism for 'hell'. The
  phrase is equivalent to 'What the heck'.
comp'ny i.e. guest.
cootie Body louse.
Burris Ewell The incident of the cootie thus serves to introduce the
  reader to the Ewell family and their 'contentious' father. In the second
  paragraph of Chapter 1 Scout has maintained 'that the Ewells started
  it all'.
kerosene American term for paraffin.
truant lady i.e. school attendance officer.
contentious Quarrelsome.

crackling bread Corn bread made with cracklings, i.e. the crisp residue left after fat or lard has been rendered.
green whisky Perhaps cheap whisky that has not been left to mature.
last-will-and-testament diction i.e. involved legal vocabulary.

Chapter 4

On her way home from school one afternoon Scout finds two pieces of chewing gum in a knot-hole of a live oak at the edge of the Radley garden. Later there are two scrubbed and polished old pennies. In the summer Dill returns and the Radley Place continues to hold its sinister fascination for the children in their games. On one of the days when they are acting the parts of the Radley family – 'a melancholy little drama' – they are caught by Atticus, who is displeased. On another occasion Scout, riding inside an old car tyre, is pushed so hard by Jem that she finishes in front of the Radley Place steps and hears the sound of Boo Radley inside, quietly laughing at their games.

half-Decimal half Dunce-cap i.e. a mixture of new and traditional methods, mingling encouragement and punishment.
Indian-heads Old American copper coins of one-cent denomination, known as 'pennies', with a design of the head of an Indian in war-dress on one side.
Cecil Jacobs He and Mrs Dubose, who is mentioned in the same sentence, both reappear later in significant episodes in the story.
scuppernongs The scuppernong is a variety of American grape (or fox-grape), named after the river in North Carolina where it first grew profusely.
slicked Polished.
six-weeks tests i.e. regular tests in school.
Bay St. Louis There is a Bay St Louis on the southern coast of Mississippi. It is not certain that this is the one referred to here.
L & N Louisville and Nashville.
In a pig's ear An expression of disbelief.
Rover Boys As in note, p.25. Their names were Tom, Sam and Dick.
Yawl You all, i.e. all of you.
reward The phrase is used ironically to mean 'get his own back'.
transparent It was easy to see what Jem was thinking.
Gothic Here the word means something like 'horrific' – originally after the novels of mystery and gloom by writers like Mrs Radcliffe and M. G. Lewis in the late eighteenth century; later applied to psychological horror-tales. (The word is used in a different sense in Chapter 15.)

Chapter 5

Somewhat neglected by Jem and Dill, Scout spends much time with Miss Maudie Atkinson, who lives across the street. She allows the children considerable freedom in her much-loved garden and often bakes cakes for them. Miss Maudie talks wisely with Scout about religion and people and tries to deflate some of her extravagant ideas about Boo Radley. Meanwhile Jem and Dill have planned to push a note to Boo Radley through the shutter, inviting him to come out and talk to them and offering to buy him an ice-cream. Their attempt is thwarted by the appearance of Atticus, who tells them firmly to stop tormenting Boo Radley and plays a 'lawyer's trick' on the protesting Jem.

coveralls American term for a boiler suit.
nut-grass A variety of American sedge, so called because its roots have nut-shaped tubers.
Second Battle of the Marne The scene, during the First World War, of one of the most powerful offences of the allied forces against the Germans, north-east of Paris, in 1918.
bridgework A bridge-like structure which supports false teeth.
Nashville The state capital of Tennessee, the state north of Alabama.
poundcake A rich sweet cake, so called because it contains a pound of each of the main ingredients.
Brigadier General Joe Wheeler An American army officer and politician (1836–1906), who was a major-general of volunteers in the Spanish-American War of 1898.

Chapter 6

On Dill's last night in Maycomb, he and Jem plan to peep through a window of the Radley Place to try to get a look at Boo Radley. Scout objects at first but then joins them, as they creep under the wire fence at the back of the Radley garden and enter the back yard. They help Dill up to the window with the loose shutter; as he can see nothing there, they move to the back porch. Jem has just crawled to a window when they are all terrified by the shadow of a man with a hat, which moves towards them, and then goes away. While they are escaping in panic they hear the roar of a shotgun. Jem has to leave his trousers, which are caught on the wire fence as he struggles beneath it.

When they have regained their breath, they stroll casually to the front pavement, to find a crowd of neighbours aroused by Mr Nathan Radley's shooting at 'a Negro' in his collard patch. Mr Radley says he has the other barrel waiting for the next sound he hears in his garden. Dill explains the absence of Jem's trousers by saying he had won them from him at strip-poker. Miss Rachel Haverford, Dill's aunt, is outraged that he should have been gambling and Jem saves him by saying that they only played with matches. After Dill has left them, Jem and Scout lie sleepless from fear that Boo Radley will seek revenge on them. Nevertheless, Jem insists on creeping back, when Atticus is asleep, to retrieve his trousers. Scout is terrified until he returns safely with the trousers.

whistled bob-white The bob-white is the American quail, so called because its song is said to sound like the two words 'bob white'. Jem's call-signal was to whistle in imitation of this.
cross [in the moon], lady in the moon Fancied figures interpreting the light and shadows in the full moon. The phrases are better known in the Southern States than our 'man in the moon'.
kudzu Ornamental plant from China and Japan, with flowers that resemble butterflies in shape.
untalented i.e. because she was a girl!
Angel May Compare Jem's earlier references to Scout as 'Miss Priss'. Angel May may have been the name of a mawkishly good character in contemporary fiction or films.
sam holy hill See note on 'what the sam hill', p.27.
Franklin stove A special kind of domestic heating stove with doors, named after its inventor, Benjamin Franklin (1706–90).
pants i.e. trousers. What the English call 'pants' are called 'shorts' by the Americans.
broken i.e. with the loading mechanism of the gun opened.
Jem fielded Dill's fly with his eyes shut He extricated them from a dangerous situation with ease, like a baseball player who takes a catch with his eyes closed. A fly, or fly ball, is a ball which has been hit up into the air and which may be easily caught 'on the fly'.

Chapter 7

Jem is silent and moody for a week after the incident in the Radley garden. He then tells Scout that when he had retrieved his trousers they had been roughly sewn and folded across the fence – 'like they were expectin' me'. Scout and Jem find a ball of grey twine in the knot-hole of the oak tree and later two small images carved in soap, a packet of chewing gum, a medal and a pocket watch and knife on a chain. The day after they leave a note of thanks Mr Nathan Radley fills the knot-hole with cement, claiming that the tree is dying – though Atticus confirms Jem's belief that this is not so.

flunked Failed.
recess Break between lessons.
hoodooing (or voodooing) The carrying out of superstitious practices, originating in African witchcraft, by Negroes of the West Indies and the southern United States. Some of these practices involved the use of effigies for casting a curse over an enemy.
bangs Front hair cut straight across the brows; in Britain, 'a fringe'.
whittles Scout misunderstands the meaning of the word and thinks of Mr Avery's feat at the beginning of Chapter 6.
poison See Jem's remarks on chewing gum in Chapter 4.
camel-kicked A camel-kick is perhaps a surreptitious sideways kick – here a warning that Scout should keep quiet.

Chapter 8

That winter (1933) old Mrs Radley dies. Atticus can give the children no information of Mr Arthur (Boo). Scout sees snow for the first time. She and Jem make a snowman, which is a caricature of Mr Avery until, on Atticus's advice, they make it look like Miss Maudie Atkinson, with her sunhat and hedge-clippers. That night Miss Maudie's house catches fire. Atticus, Mr Avery and the other men of Maycomb help, while Jem and Scout are told to stand in front of the Radley Place and watch. As they do so, they become colder and colder.

By dawn Miss Maudie's home has been completely destroyed. Scout finds a woollen blanket round her shoulders and they realize it had been put there by Boo Radley, without their seeing him. They are horrified to think that if Scout had happened to turn round she would have actually seen the terrifying Boo Radley. Next morning the children clear away the snowman and find that Miss Maudie takes a remarkably philosophical view of the loss of her home.

Rosetta Stone This tablet of black basalt (now in the British Museum) was discovered in 1799, near Rosetta in the Nile Delta. It had been erected in 195 BC in honour of one of the Ptolemies. The inscription was in three languages and was the means by which Egyptian hieroglyphics were first deciphered. Mr Avery's ideas of the inscription are, of course, quite wrong.

cannas As in note, p.25.

touchous i.e. touchy, easily angered.

twitch Hunch, intuitive feeling.

Appomattox The American Civil War was virtually ended by the surrender of General Lee to General Grant in 1865 at a village in Virginia called Appomattox Court-house.

performance A reference to the incident at the beginning of Chapter 6.

thrift Sea-pink, a small plant often used to decorate the edges of garden borders.

burlap Coarse canvas.

jim-dandy Wonderful.

morphodite A shortened and altered form of 'hermaphrodite' – literally a creature having both male and female characteristics; here, a being that might be of either sex. The 'snowman' had resembled both Mr Avery and Miss Maudie.

hon An abbreviation of 'honey'.

he's crazy The 'he' here is Arthur (Boo) Radley, not Mr Nathan.

roomers i.e. lodgers.

Bellingraths The Bellingrath Gardens in Theodore, near Mobile, are famous for their beauty and the profusion of their flowers.

stove up Suffering physical discomfort caused by injury.

Chapter 9

Scout is taunted almost to fighting by Cecil Jacobs, who says her father is 'defending niggers'. Atticus tries to explain to her why he has taken on the case of the Black Tom Robinson and persuades her to take a rational rather than emotional view of things, forbidding her to engage in fighting. Her resolution holds out until Christmas. When Uncle Jack visits them, he reprimands Scout for swearing; he brings air rifles as presents for Jem and herself. All four, as is their custom, spend Christmas at Finch's Landing.

The family homestead is now ruled by Aunt Alexandra, who thinks that Scout is not being properly brought up. Scout is uncomfortable in this conventional and strictly run household. She finds her sanctimonious cousin Francis a special trial and is in serious trouble when she attacks him for calling Atticus and herself 'nigger-lovers'. For Atticus's sake Scout does not reveal the nature of her provocation, even when this leads to a serious misunderstanding with Uncle Jack. Back at home, Scout overhears a conversation between Atticus and Uncle Jack about herself. They discuss the way to handle children and Atticus's anxiety about his children during the difficult time of the coming trial of Tom Robinson. Only later does Scout realize that Atticus wanted her to overhear his words.

still Apparatus for distilling liquor. 'Running a still' without a licence was illegal, of course.

Confederate veteran One who had been a soldier in the army of the Confederate States in the American Civil War (1861–5).

General Hood A Confederate general (1831–79) in the American Civil War.

Missouri Compromise This consists of a number of legal bills of the United States Congress which were necessary before Missouri, one of the slave states, could finally be admitted as the twenty-fourth state in 1820.

Stonewall Jackson The nickname of Thomas Jonathan Jackson (b. 1824), an American general who joined the Southern (Confederate) army on the outbreak of the Civil War. He died in May 1863; hence Cousin Ike's apology for his error.

Ol' Blue Light Another nickname for General Jackson.

Yankees Inhabitants of the northern United States.

drew a bead on i.e. 'took aim at'.

Rose Aylmer The cat was named after the main character of a poem by W. S. Landor (1775–1864).

catwalk Narrow footway, usually high up along the side of a building.

widow's walk 'A railed observation platform built above the roof of a coastal dwelling for an unobstructed outlook to sea' (Webster).

booksack i.e. satchel.

ambrosia A dessert of a fruit or mixed fruits topped with shredded coconut.

runt Undersized person.

sass i.e. sauce, behave or speak impertinently towards.

Hodge The name of Dr Johnson's cat. The other details, mentioned in the same sentence, also refer to Samuel Johnson (1709–84), the great English man of letters. 'Boswell's marvellous *Life* has made Johnson's bodily appearance, dress and manners more familiar to posterity than those of any other man' (*Everyman's Dictionary of Literary Biography*).

romped on her Dealt with her harshly.

Lord Melbourne The 'old Prime Minister' of the previous page. This English statesmen (1778–1848) was Prime Minister from 1834 until 1841.

Jem keeping his head Ironically, it is Jem who breaks out before Scout, in Chapter 11, when he damages Mrs Dubose's camellia bushes.

the Ewells Once again we are reminded of a name that is to assume a major significance later in the story.

Chapter 10

Jem and Scout feel that Atticus has none of the impressive attributes of other fathers and neither Miss Maudie Atkinson nor Calpurnia really succeeds in convincing Scout that he has many outstanding abilities. When they have their air rifles Atticus says they may shoot jays but they must remember it is a sin to kill a mockingbird; he leaves them to be taught the rudiments of shooting by Uncle Jack, who says Atticus has no interest in guns.

One day in February Jem and Scout come across a mad dog (Tim Johnson). They inform Calpurnia, who telephones Atticus and warns the neighbourhood, even running to the Radley Place. When Atticus and Mr Heck Tate, the sheriff of Maycomb County, arrive with a heavy rifle, the sheriff insists that only Atticus is capable of taking the difficult shot. Atticus shoots the dog dead in front of the Radley gate and Jem and Scout are greatly impressed. When they learn that their father was once known as One-Shot Finch, the children are even more impressed by their father's modesty.

keep-away American term for a goalkeeper.
bluejays American jays.
mockingbird An American bird of the thrush family, with a habit of mocking other birds' songs and other sounds.
corncribs Mangers, fodder-racks.
checker-player Checkers is another name for the game of draughts.
coming up Growing up.
going out Playing in the team.
bird dog One that has been trained to retrieve birds for hunters.
Sheriff In the United States the sheriff is the chief executive officer of the county, his principal duties being to maintain peace and order, attend courts, guard prisoners, serve processes and carry out the judgments of the courts.
mockingbirds were silent The apprehension of this silent waiting is later recalled at a significant moment in Chapter 21.
moseyin' Moving along slowly.
one-shot job They would have to kill the mad dog with the first shot.
had my 'druthers Had a choice. 'Druther is a corruption of 'would rather'.
Zeebo Calpurnia's son, the garbage collector.

Chapter 11

Mrs Henry Lafayette Dubose, who lives two doors to the north of the Finch family, is old, irritable and hard to please, and regularly expresses her very low opinion of Jem and Scout. One day she is particularly vicious in her outspoken attack on them, their family and their father: this is the first time an adult has insulted Atticus for defending a Black. On their return from town, Jem is unable to restrain himself any longer: he rushes wildly into Mrs Dubose's garden and cuts off every single flower on her camellia bushes.

When Atticus returns home that evening Jem is sent to apologize to Mrs Dubose, while Atticus explains to Scout how he would be unable to live with his own conscience if he failed to defend Tom Robinson. Jem has to work in Mrs Dubose's garden every Saturday and, with Scout, has to read to her for two hours after school every day for a month. Atticus explains that Mrs Dubose is a very sick woman and that the term 'nigger-lover' reflects more on those that use it than on those to whom they apply it. At each visit Mrs Dubose keeps Jem reading longer and longer. A month after their last visit, Mrs Dubose dies, and Atticus explains how, during her last months, she had been trying to overcome her addiction to morphine. Jem's reading sessions had helped her to do so and her last gift, a perfect white camellia blossom, upsets him. Atticus, however, explains Mrs Dubose's motives and her particular kind of courage.

passé Out of fashion.
real property i.e. real estate (land, with the buildings, fences etc., upon it) as distinct from personal and movable property.
dog-trot hall Also called a 'breeze-way' – this is a roofed passage or porch with open sides.
CSA Confederate States of America.
sassiest Cheekiest, most impertinent.
mutts Blockheads.
Playing hooky i.e. playing truant.
scuppernong see note, p.28.
lawing Defending in court.
trash Worthless persons, members of an inferior social group.
philippic Violent speech of abuse (after the speeches of the Greek orator Demosthenes against Philip of Macedon).
guff Nonsense, humbug.
Dixie Howell A star ball-carrier in the football team of the University of Alabama.

relic The pistol that Mrs Dubose was rumoured to possess.
calomel Mercurious chloride, used as a purgative medicine.
'druthers As in note p.34.
Ivanhoe The most popular of the Waverley novels of Sir Walter Scott (1771–1832).
water dippers Vessels with long handles for dipping into drinking water.
Snow-on-the-Mountain Mrs Dubose is referring to a species of her camellias. (In England it is the popular name for a species of Arabis, a white rock plant.)
Rose Bowl A large stadium in Pasadena, California, in which the final of the American national football championship is played.
a man with a gun Atticus is implying that the fight to establish Tom Robinson's innocence will be a far more difficult task than shooting a mad dog.

Revision questions on Part 1

1 Write a brief but lively description of each of the members of the Finch family other than Atticus, Scout and Jem.

2 Write an account of the games that Jem and Scout play with Dill.

3 Say what you know about the Cunninghams.

4 Write a lively description of each of the following neighbours: (a) Mr Avery, (b) Mrs Dubose, (c) Miss Maudie Atkinson.

5 What are the really important things that Scout learned at school on her first day?

6 Write an account of the episodes in the story so far which involve the Radley Place as they appear to Jem, Scout and Dill. What is the real significance of these episodes?

7 Write an account of the fire which burnt down Miss Maudie Atkinson's house.

8 Describe the Christmas visit to Finch's Landing.

9 Write an account of the episode involving Tim Johnson, the mad dog. What do you learn from this episode of Atticus's character?

10 Why does Mrs Dubose make Jem read to her?

Part 2
Chapter 12

Jem, now twelve, is experiencing the uncertainties of growing up and Scout, who spends more time with Calpurnia, begins 'to think there is some skill involved in being a girl'. She is sad when she learns that this year her childhood 'sweetheart', Dill, who now has a new father, will not be able to spend the summer in Maycomb.

While Atticus attends a session of the state legislature the children are looked after by Calpurnia, who, one Sunday, takes them with her to a service at the Negro Methodist Episcopal Church. Jem and Scout are welcomed with great respect by all except a Black woman called Lula. They are fascinated by a form of service unfamiliar to them and by the Reverend Sykes's method of augmenting the collection. They learn that Bob Ewell has had Tom Robinson arrested on a charge of raping his daughter. Calpurnia tells them how she learned to read from a textbook on law; they discuss her 'modest double life' – with the Finch household and with her own people – and learn something of her simple wisdom.

Birmingham This is Birmingham, Alabama, of course – an important industrial town of Jefferson County, about 224 km (140 miles) north of Monroeville.

bread lines An American term for the queues of poor and starving people waiting for free food or relief, distributed from state sources.

Shadrach Shadrach, Meshach and Abednego were three Jews whom Nebuchadnezzar, the King of Babylon, ordered to be cast into 'a burning fiery furnace' as a punishment for refusing to worship a golden image. See Daniel 3.

Octagon soap The brand name of a kind of laundry soap. The cake of soap had the four corners cut off to give it a distinctive shape with eight sides.

castile i.e. castile soap, made with olive-oil and soda.

Mardi Gras The last day of the pre-Lent carnival, celebrated with all sorts of festivities on Shrove Tuesday.

M.E. Methodist Episcopal.

Quarters Town district inhabited by the Blacks.

asafoetida A resinous gum with a strong smell of garlic.

comp'ny Guests.

Hunt William Holman Hunt (1827–1910) was an English painter, who, with Millais and Rossetti, founded the group of painters known as the pre-Raphaelite Brotherhood. His painting *The Light of the World* depicts Christ as a shepherd with a lantern.

lined Called out the words, line by line.

Blackstone's _Commentaries_ Sir William Blackstone (1723–80) was a lawyer and lecturer on law who became the first Vinerian professor of law at Oxford. His famous _Commentaries on the Laws of England_, in three volumes, was at one time the main textbook of English law.

to beat Moses Perhaps to gain a spiritual advantage.

Chapter 13

Aunt Alexandra arrives to look after the children and to provide 'some feminine influence' and Maycomb welcomes her and her multifarious activities. She is full of moral fervour and has a highly developed sense of social status – an attitude for which some aspects of Maycomb's history provide support. Atticus finds it hard to share her exaggerated sense of family pride and 'gentle breeding'; he becomes decidedly uncomfortable when, at Alexandra's insistence, he tries to play the role of conventional father by explaining to his children the 'proper' behaviour expected of Finches.

shinny This is some kind of alcoholic drink.

Rice Christians People who become converts to Christianity for the material benefits they gain thereby (e.g. Indians who were given a supply of rice).

Amanuensis Club A literary group, probably for the encouragement of amateur journalism.

Penfield A family name, perhaps.

pig-trails Trails by which pigs were driven to market.

Creek Nation A confederacy of Indian tribes originally occupying territory north of Florida before the establishment of the State of Alabama in 1819.

Lydia E. Pinkham bottles Lydia E. Pinkham was a brand name for a group of patent medicines; originally they were mainly for female disorders.

mandrake There are many superstitions connected with the root of the mandrake, or mandragora. In the southern states of America some of these beliefs may well have been linked with changelings – children exchanged for others by supernatural means. The idea of changelings in relation to Aunt Alexandra had occurred earlier in Scout's mind in Chapter 9.

redbug A kind of harvest-tick in America.

Chapter 14

Jem and Scout become more and more aware of the towns-people's gossip about the Finch family as a result of their father's involvement with the Robinson case. They are also aware that their aunt's views on bringing up children differ very much from those of their father. Jem realizes that the Robinson case is causing Atticus a great deal of worry; however, the superior way in which Jem lectures Scout provokes a fight between brother and sister. What Scout thinks might be a snake under her bed that evening turns out to be Dill. Jem takes a responsible attitude towards Dill's sudden appearance and calls Atticus who arranges for him to stay in Maycomb. Dill explains to Scout that he has run away from home because he feels his mother and new father are just not interested in him. When Scout wonders why Boo Radley has never run away, Dill says that perhaps he had nowhere to go.

Yessum i.e. yes, ma'am.
morphodite As in note, p.32. Clearly Scout has no real understanding of the word.
rattler i.e. rattlesnake, the poisonous American pit-viper. (The 'rattle' is made by the horny rings on its tail.)
corn bread Bread made of maize meal.
this narrative This is Dill's imaginary story. In answer to Jem's repetition of the question 'How'd you get here?' Dill tells what really happened.

Chapter 15

A group of Maycomb citizens visit Atticus one Saturday evening to tell him they fear there will be trouble when Tom Robinson is moved to the Maycomb jail: Jem begins to feel great concern for his father's safety. Late the following night, after Atticus has gone out, taking with him an electric light bulb, Jem, accompanied by Scout and Dill, creeps from home and goes into town. The children find Atticus sitting reading outside the jail by the light of the bare bulb on an extension cord. Having satisfied themselves about their father's safety, the children are about to move quietly away when a number of cars appear. Atticus is soon surrounded by a crowd of threatening Cunninghams, who have come to lynch Tom Robinson. Fearing danger, Scout pushes forward and Jem defies his father's instructions to take her home. When a man grabs Jem by the collar Scout kicks him; her personal appeal to the father of Walter Cunningham and her concern about his entailment embarrasses him but succeeds in bringing the other men to their senses as they recall Atticus's value to the community. One by one they shuffle away. Tom Robinson settles down to a peaceful night inside the jail, as Mr Underwood, editor of the *Maycomb Tribune*, reveals that he had kept Atticus covered with his double-barrelled shotgun. Atticus is grateful to his children.

Old Sarum bunch i.e. the Cunninghams.

shinnied up The worse for drink.

Henry W. Grady A celebrated journalist, newspaper editor and orator, Grady (1850–89) made a number of famous speeches which helped to reconcile animosities after the Civil War.

chair i.e. the electric chair.

Ku Klux The Ku Klux Klan was originally a secret social club of young white men at the close of the Civil War in a town in Tennessee. It rapidly increased in numbers until it became an organization to oppose the abolition of Black slavery and to work for the suppression of the Blacks by murder and terrorism. In 1871 it was suppressed by Congress; it was revived in 1915 in Georgia and quickly spread throughout the southern states; but, defeated by its own extreme violence, the Ku Klux Klan died out in the late 1920s. (After the Civil Rights Act of 1964 there was a revival of Klan activity in some southern states in an attempt to oppose measures towards desegregation.)

bob-white See note, p.30.

johnson grass See note, p.25.

Gothic A style of architecture characterized by clustered columns and high-pointed arches.

Jitney Jungle Jitney is American slang for 'nickel', a five-cent piece. Jitney Jungle is probably the name of an entertainment arcade.

somebody's man . . . jumped See the paragraph in which 'checkerboard' was mentioned earlier in this chapter.

You're damn tootin' they won't You're damn right they won't.

Chapter 16

At breakfast the following morning, Atticus explains how Mr Cunningham, at heart a friend of the Finches, had been influenced by the mob. However, the children's actions caused him to stop and reflect on his actions. Throughout the morning there is a steady influx of people into Maycomb for the trial of

Tom Robinson; after dinner Jem, Scout and Dill head for the town, which is crowded as if for a gala. They are particularly fascinated by the sight of Mr Dolphus Raymond, a white man who lives with the Blacks. They go with the crowds which sweep into the courtroom and join the Reverend Sykes in the 'Coloured' balcony. We are told of a former encounter of Judge Taylor with the Cunninghams.

pushing up his glasses The reference is to the episode of the mad dog in Chapter 10.

Braxton Bragg Bragg (1817–76) was a brave but not very successful Confederate general.

Mennonites Members of a Protestant sect whose beliefs combined some of those of the Baptists and the Quakers. They were called Mennonites after the name of one of their founders, Menno Simons (1492–1559). The sect is still active in Holland and Germany, as well as in the United States.

William Jennings Bryan An American politician (1860–1925) with a great reputation as a public speaker.

popped-the-whip A reference to a children's game in which the players join hands in a line and run. The leader swings the line in one direction and then suddenly the other way, so that those at the end have to run very fast in order to avoid being thrown down.

crackers i.e. biscuits.

Nehi Cola The trade name of a soft drink flavoured with cola nuts. The name was meant to suggest that the bottle was so big that it came up to your knee.

Arlington The reference may be to the famous mansion in the Arlington National Cemetery, near Washington, D.C. It was built on the estate of George Washington's adopted son and its portico with eight white columns is a well-known landmark.

Champertous connivance A private understanding by which one party assists another in a law suit and then has a share of the proceeds. (The technical term 'champertous' is a legacy of Norman French.)

Chapter 17

Heck Tate, the sheriff, is called to testify. He tells the court how one night he was called to the Ewell home, where Bob Ewell's daughter Mayella claimed to have been raped by Tom Robinson. In his questioning of the sheriff, Atticus emphasizes the facts that Mayella's injuries were mainly on the right side of her face and all round her throat and that no doctor was called. The next witness is Bob Ewell himself, a mean little man from a decrepit little cabin near the Black quarter of town. The coarseness of his language in his accusation against Tom Robinson disrupts the court. Atticus's questions to the witness suggest that Ewell has no real concern for Mayella; and Atticus also establishes that Ewell is left-handed. (The position of Mayella's facial injuries suggested that they had been caused by a left-handed person.)

title dispute A dispute about the right to possession of property.
namesake General Robert E. Lee (1807–70) was commander-in-chief of the Confederate army during the American Civil War.
shingled Covered with thick flat pieces used like roofing-slates.
shotgun i.e. as in a 'shot-gun house' in which all the rooms are in direct line with each other, usually front to back.
varmints Vermin.
possum Colloquial for opossum, a species of mammal, about the size of a large cat, which is very common in the United States.
ruttin' on Copulating with. Ewell's expression is usually applied to animals.
slung In disorder, with everything flung about.
frog-sticking without a light i.e. not having taken sufficient precaution.
Sherlock Holmes The famous private detective who is the central character in so many stories and novels by Sir A. Conan Doyle (1859–1930).

Chapter 18

The next witness, Mayella Ewell, is afraid and at first bursts into tears. Reassured by Judge Taylor, Mayella gives her testimony. When Atticus questions her, she claims he is making fun of her because he addresses her as 'ma'am' and 'Miss Mayella'. His questions slowly build up a picture of the Ewells' pathetic home life, Mayella's loneliness and the shortcomings of Ewell as a father. Atticus's later questions cast serious doubts on parts of Mayella's testimony and even suggest that she was beaten up by her father. Tom Robinson's left arm and hand are useless as the result of an accident when he was a boy.

Has she got good sense? Is she all there?
chiffarobe A piece of furniture which has both drawers and space to hang clothes.
sass i.e. sauce, impertinence.
sassed Spoken to disrespectfully.

Mr Jingle A character in Dickens's *Pickwick Papers*, who spoke in short disconnected phrases.

ground-itch A skin complaint.

tollable i.e. tolerable.

paw i.e. pa.

led by the nose as asses are Following with docility the suggestions or guidance of a stronger character. The phrase is originally used by Iago of Othello in Shakespeare's *Othello*, I,3.

Chapter 19

Atticus's only witness is the defendant Tom Robinson, who reveals that Mayella Ewell had invited him inside her fence many times to do various chores for her. Scout realizes that poor Mayella must have been even lonelier than Boo Radley. Tom's account of the events at the Ewell house on the November evening in question is very different from Mayella's. According to Tom's testimony, Mayella, after ensuring that her brothers and sisters were not at home, had taken the initiative and embraced Tom, who had then fled. At the end of Tom's testimony, his employer, Mr Link Deas, rises to praise the defendant and is summarily dismissed from the courtroom by Judge Taylor. Mr Gilmer, Ewell's solicitor, tries to discredit Tom and questions him harshly, especially when Tom says he did chores for Mayella because he felt sorry for her. Dill is upset by this and Scout takes him outside; there they see Mr Link Deas and talk with Mr Dolphus Raymond.

pecan See note, p.25.

fall i.e. autumn.

slap Whole, complete.

seb'm i.e. seven.

ugly Rough, causing embarrassment.

ex cathedra Uttered with authority. The phrase originally applied to pronouncements made by the Pope from his throne; it is sometimes used ironically to describe a dogmatic assertion.

boy A black servant or labourer of any age was often called 'boy' to emphasize his inferior social position.

buck i.e. a black male (derogatory).

didn't go to be Did not intend to be.

He's the same ... public streets Miss Maudie Atkinson uses a similar phrase in Chapter 5.

Chapter 20

When Mr Dolphus Raymond shares his drink with Dill, he and
Scout discover it is merely Coca-Cola and not the whisky every-
one believes he drinks. He explains why he pretends to be worse
than he is and talks of 'the simple hell people give other people'.
They return to the courtroom to hear the second half of
Atticus's speech to the jury, in which he talks of the rigid code of
a society which governs the relations of black and white. It is
Mayella's guilt at breaking this code which puts Tom Robinson's
life at stake. Atticus attacks those who cynically believe that all
Blacks are basically immoral and reminds the jury that all men
are equal before the law. A court is only as sound as its jury, and
a jury is only as sound as those whom it comprises. Atticus urges
them to restore Tom Robinson to his family.

Thomas Jefferson American statesman (1743–1826) and third
President of the United States. He drew up the draft of the
Declaration of Independence in 1776, from which the phrase 'All men
are created equal' is taken.
distaff side Female part. The reference is probably to the work of the
wife of the President of the United States at that time.
Washington This city, in the District of Columbia, is the capital of the
United States.
Rockefeller John D. Rockefeller (1839–1937), one of the founders of
the Standard Oil Company, became one of the richest men in the
world and on his retirement devoted his wealth to philanthropic work.
Einstein Albert Einstein (1879–1955), physicist, famous for his work
on the theory of relativity. After several academic positions in
Switzerland and Germany, he taught at Princeton, in the United
States.

Chapter 21

Calpurnia is sent by Aunt Alexandra to the courtroom to tell
Atticus that the children are missing. They are discovered and
taken home. After supper they return to the courtroom, where
Jem discusses the possible verdict with the Reverend Sykes.
After several hours the jury delivers its verdict: Tom Robinson is
found guilty. As Atticus leaves the courtroom all the Blacks
stand out of respect for him.

gettin' some kinda head Becoming more mature and thoughtful.
giving her precious Jem down the country i.e. withdrawing her

protection, betraying him. Like 'selling down the river', the phrase originates from the days of the slave trade.

biblical patience Job, for instance, is the personification of patience. His story is told in the Bible in the Book of Job.

a cold February morning The reference is to the moments of silent apprehension in the mad-dog episode in Chapter 10.

Chapter 22

Jem weeps from disappointment and when Aunt Alexandra doubts the wisdom of her brother's having allowed the children to attend the trial Atticus argues that this is 'just as much Maycomb as missionary teas'. Next morning their kitchen table is loaded with gifts of food from Black families.

Miss Stephanie Crawford and Mr Avery do nothing but gossip but Miss Maudie Atkinson senses that, in growing up, Jem is beginning to experience disillusionment; she expresses her sympathy for the children and her admiration for Atticus. Miss Maudie points out that it was no accident that Judge Taylor named Atticus to defend Tom Robinson and the fact that the jury took so long to reach a verdict was at least one small step forward. Dill's disillusion leads him to announce that, since there is nothing he can do about people except laugh, he will join the circus as a clown. The children learn that Bob Ewell has that morning spat in Atticus's face and said that he will 'get him'.

White House Residence of the President of the United States, in Washington, D.C.

scuppernongs See note, p.28.

runner Chicken leg, perhaps.

bridgework As in note, p.29.

Chapter 23

Atticus takes Bob Ewell's threat very calmly but Jem and Scout are afraid on his account. Atticus allays their fears, however, by explaining Ewell's motives, and says that Ewell's spitting in his face is better than his beating Mayella. They await the result of an appeal to a higher court and Jem and Atticus discuss legal points. Atticus has less faith than Jem in the power of reason and he fears that one day they must pay the price for low-grade white men constantly taking advantage of so-called Black ignorance. But he sees the fact that the jury took so long to reach its verdict as 'the shadow of a beginning' of a better situation. Atticus reveals that one of the jurymen who was for an outright acquittal was a member of the Cunningham family. Scout's resolve to be kind to Walter Cunningham is discouraged by Aunt Alexandra. All in all, Scout and Jem find it very difficult to understand 'folks' and Jem thinks he begins to understand why Boo Radley stays shut up in the house – he just *wants* to.

peace bond A court order to keep the peace.

Chester County A fictitious name.

pay the bill for it Atticus's fears for the future (which are really those of Miss Harper Lee, writing her novel in Alabama just prior to 1960) were fully justified. The Civil Rights movement and the beginnings of the fight for equality for Blacks were closely related to the situation in Alabama and were led by the Reverend Martin Luther King, at one time a minister in Montgomery. In December 1955 the Blacks had organized a peaceful boycott of buses to protest against segregation. Later, unhappily, the protests of the Civil Rights movement were met with the kind of violence that is now permanently associated with the names Selma and Birmingham, Alabama.

rarin' Eager.

hung jury A jury that is prevented from reaching a unanimous decision because one member refuses to join in a verdict.

Gee minetti American slang has many expressions of surprise and emphasis which begin with 'gee'. It has been suggested that originally perhaps this was a corruption of 'Jesus'.

distant disastrous occasion The occasion was Scout's first day at school. See Chapter 2.

yappy Uncouth.

yap Uncouth or ignorant person.

tacky i.e. an inferior or low-class person.

Cajuns People of mixed white, Indian, and Negro ancestry in south-west Alabama and adjoining sections of Mississippi.

Baldwin County One of the two southernmost counties of the state of Alabama, lying between Mobile Bay and the state boundary with Florida.

pot-liquor A thin broth in which meat has been boiled.

hipped on Obsessed by.

Chapter 24

Jem has learned much from his discussions with Atticus; Scout is now to learn much from the ladies of Maycomb. She helps at one of her aunt's Missionary Circle tea-parties and is treated with understanding and guidance by Miss Maudie Atkinson. Mrs Grace Merriweather shows concern for the distant Mrunas but she and Mrs Gertrude Farrow adopt a very superficial and patronizing attitude towards the Blacks nearer home (and Helen Robinson in particular) with some veiled criticism of Atticus. Miss Maudie icily punctures their pretentiousness. Scout feels less at home with the deviousness of 'the world of ladies' than the straightforward world of men.

Atticus arrives home early with the news that Tom Robinson has been shot dead while trying to escape from Enfield Prison Farm; he takes Calpurnia with him when he goes to see Helen Robinson. Aunt Alexandra, anxious about the strain under which Atticus is living at present, is sustained by Miss Maudie's wise and comforting words, and her view that Atticus is supported by a handful of enlightened citizens of Maycomb. Scout learns that being a 'lady' involves forgetting one's personal troubles.

charlotte A dessert made by lining a dish with strips of bread, cake or sponge cakes and filling it with fruit, whipped cream, custard or any other filling.
Mrunas, it sounded like to me It is not clear that such a name really exists.
when their time came i.e. when they were about to give birth.
yaws A contagious disease of the skin.
dewberry A kind of bramble or blackberry, so named because of the dew-like bloom on the fruit.
the preacher's wife ... yet i.e. is pregnant.
up there i.e. in the northern states.
Mrs Roosevelt Mrs Eleanor Roosevelt (1884–1962), wife of Franklin D. Roosevelt, President of the United States from 1933 to 1945, was an indefatigable worker in liberal causes and in the field of human rights.
cookies Biscuits.

Chapter 25

Scout is puzzled by the way Jem's wide charity has now embraced the insect world. She recalls how Jem and Dill, returning from swimming, had met Atticus and been allowed to accompany him on his visit to Helen Robinson to tell of Tom's death. Maycomb's interest in Tom's death is short-lived and soon gives way to glib generalizations about Blacks. Mr Underwood, however, writes a bitter editorial in the *Maycomb Tribune*:

the death of Tom Robinson, he says, is like the senseless slaughter of songbirds by hunters and children, a meaningless sacrifice to ignorance. Meanwhile, Bob Ewell is still hinting at reprisals against the Finch family.

lightning bugs Fireflies.
night crawlers Large earthworms which come to the surface at night.
roly-poly Kind of wood-louse.
redbug See note, p.38.
English Channel The metaphor is justified by the large volume of
  shipping in the Channel.

Chapter 26

Now in the third grade at school, Scout recalls the game of making Boo Radley come out. The Radley Place is no less gloomy than it was but it is no longer a cause of terror. Scout can even imagine meeting Arthur Radley quite casually on his front porch. She senses that there is a certain strain in her relations with the people of Maycomb as a result of Atticus's part in the Robinson case. She concludes that people are peculiar and is quite content to withdraw from them, until the subject of Hitler's treatment of the Jews comes up at school in one of Miss Gates's Current Events periods. Scout cannot understand how Miss Gates can hate Hitler so intensely when she recalls hearing her say (on the night of Tom Robinson's trial) that the Blacks must be made to know their place. When she discusses this with Jem he flies into a rage and says he never wants to be reminded of the court-house. Atticus asks Scout to be patient with Jem, who hasn't got things sorted out yet.

collards As in note, p.24.
a couple of times The reader will no doubt recall when these were. See
  Chapters 6 and 8.
You were lucky Atticus is referring to the incident related in Chapter
  6.
holy-roller A member of a minor religious sect in the USA and Canada
  whose meetings were often characterized by frenzied excitement.
Elmer Davis Davis (1890–1958) was an American radio commentator
  and author, who became a radio news analyst for the Columbia
  Broadcasting system in 1939.
Adolf Hitler In Germany Hitler (1889–1945) built up the National
  Socialist ('Nazi') party, increasing his power as a politician. As

Chancellor from 1933 onwards, he established an absolute dictatorship, which he maintained with a system of terror and ever widening territorial demands. (This was the period of the supposed events of *To Kill a Mockingbird*, the date of the present chapter being September 1935.) It took the Second World War to destroy Hitler's dictatorship, under which Jews, regarded by Hitler as the personification of evil, were first deprived of human rights and later ruthlessly destroyed.

washin' No doubt the original newspaper item said 'wiping out', or perhaps 'liquidating'.

Chapter 27

Bob Ewell continues to make accusations against Atticus, tries to break into Judge Taylor's house and intimidates Helen Robinson (though the forthright words of Helen's employer, Mr Link Deas, soon put a stop to that). For Halloween (in order to avoid anything like the practical joke that had been played on the Barber sisters the previous year) the Maycomb ladies make special arrangements that involve the children of the town. Scout, in a costume of chicken wire and painted cloth, is to represent a ham in a pageant composed by Mrs Grace Merriweather. On the evening of the performance Atticus and Aunt Alexandra (who experiences a momentary premonition) both excuse themselves from attending and Jem escorts Scout to the high-school auditorium. 'Thus began our longest journey together.'

WPA As in note, p.27.

chunked Threw things.

National Recovery Act Franklin D. Roosevelt became President in 1933, at a time of serious economic crisis. Among the many measures that comprised the programme known as the New Deal was a National Recovery Act. At first it helped recovery but later became ineffective and was repealed by the Supreme Court.

nine old men i.e. the United States Supreme Court, which consisted of a chief justice and eight associate judges.

Halloween In pre-Christian times witches and warlocks were believed to hold their revels on the night of 31 October. Though the Christian church regarded it as the eve of All Hallows or All Saints, it is still the occasion for games in which the old customs survive.

buggy In America this was a one-horse vehicle with four wheels and a single seat.

Misses Tutti and Frutti Barber Tutti-frutti (Italian for 'all fruits') is the name for ice-cream flavoured with different kinds of fruit.

Clanton A town in Chilton County, about 144 km (90 miles) north of Monroeville.

dog Victrolas Victrola is the trade name of a certain make of gramophone ('phonograph') in America but is frequently used for 'phonograph' generally. The dog listening to an early gramophone with a large horn figures as the trade mark of His Master's Voice.

apple-bobbing A game in which the contestants snatch with their mouths at apples floating on water.

taffy-pulling Taffy is a sweet made usually of molasses or brown sugar boiled until caramelized and pulled until porous and light-coloured.

Ad Astra Per Aspera Later Mrs Merriweather says, 'That means from the mud to the stars'. *Aspera* is Latin, not for 'mud', but for 'rough, harsh'.

walked over my grave This expression is often used when someone is seized with an involuntary shuddering, an experience which is regarded as a premonition.

Chapter 28

Jem and Scout (with her ham costume) walk through the darkness, past the Radley Place and across the school grounds, where Cecil Jacobs gives them a fright. While Jem joins his own friends, Scout and Cecil sample the various entertainments and sideshows (with the exception of apple-bobbing, which Cecil regards as insanitary). The history of Maycomb County is presented through Mrs Merriweather's pageant, which Scout finds so tedious that she falls asleep and misses her cue, making her entrance late at an inappropriate moment. Jem consoles her tactfully as they walk home.

In the darkness, they hear footsteps following them and at first they think Cecil Jacobs is playing another trick on them. Very soon they are attacked. Scout, hampered by her costume, hears the sound of struggling, Jem's scream and, later, the sound of a man panting and coughing. In the silence that follows she encounters a man's body on the ground and, after walking towards the road, sees in the light of a street lamp another man carrying Jem, whose arm is dangling in front of him. As soon as they reach home Atticus telephones for Dr Reynolds and the sheriff. The doctor finds that Jem, unconscious, has a broken arm and the sheriff finds under a tree the dead body of Bob Ewell with a kitchen knife between his ribs. Scout does not recognize the man who has brought Jem in.

Bet nobody bothers them Notice the irony of this.

haints Ghosts.

mocker i.e. mockingbird.

bluejay As in note, p.34.

Poor Will The American night-jar, a smaller bird then the whippoor-will (or goatsucker). The name is an attempted representation of the sound of its call.

crap games Gambling games played with two dice.

slicked-up Tidied up.

divinity i.e. divinity fudge which is made from the whites of eggs, white or brown sugar, and nuts.

climbers People bent on their own social advancement.

taffy See note on 'taffy-pulling', p.50.

mashed Crushed.

Colonel Maycomb A fictitious character.

Andrew Jackson See note on 'Andrew Jackson', p.23.

hock Jem's joke refers to Scout's costume – hock is part of the hindleg of an animal.

dangling crazily See the opening sentence of the novel.

ten forevers i.e. what seemed to be a very long time.

chinaberry As in note, p.25.

Chapter 29

Scout tells the sheriff of the walk home and he says that the chicken-wire foundation of her costume probably saved her life when Bob Ewell attacked her. She believes Jem saved her by pulling Ewell away from her and talks of the man who carried Jem home, the man who now stands before her. Suddenly, with tears in her eyes, she knows who he is – Boo Radley.

I had a feeling about this See note to 'walked over my grave' opposite.

Chapter 30

Scout treats 'Mr Arthur' with unaffected courtesy as they join Atticus and Mr Tate on the front porch. Atticus is under the impression that Jem killed Ewell in self-defence. However, when Mr Tate says Jem never stabbed Ewell, Atticus believes the sheriff is trying to protect Jem, and says the whole thing must be brought out into the open in court: it would be a denial of Atticus's principles and the way he has brought up his children if this affair were hushed up. Mr Tate claimed that Ewell fell on his knife, the kitchen knife (though it is clear now, to both Mr

Tate and Atticus, that Ewell was killed by Boo Radley). The sheriff is deliberately mysterious about a switch-blade knife he has found and is determined that Boo Radley's part in the events of the night shall not be publicized. Boo Radley has, after all, saved the lives of Jem and Scout and rid the town of a menace, and to drag a man of his shy ways into the limelight would, the sheriff believes, be a sin. Scout adds that it would be like shooting a mockingbird and, as they go inside, Atticus thanks Arthur Radley on behalf of his children.

scat Be off!

My small fantasy See Chapter 26, the paragraph beginning, 'But I still looked for him'.

one way in town The consistent moral attitude of Atticus has been several times underlined in the story. See note on 'He's the same . . .', p.43.

switch-blade knife A pocket-knife with a spring-operated blade so that pressure on a release catch causes it to fly open.

The son— He is going to say 'son of a bitch'.

not thinking of Jem— But of Boo Radley.

craw Stomach.

kitchen knife Mr Tate prefers that not everything about the two knives is made clear. The suggestion is that the kitchen knife in Ewell's stomach was Boo Radley's. According to Miss Stephanie Crawford, another domestic 'weapon' (scissors) had played a part in the early stages of Boo Radley's story.

Chapter 31

Arthur affectionately takes his leave of Jem, now sleeping peacefully, and Scout accompanies him back to his home. Standing on the Radley porch, in front of the shuttered window, Scout imagines all the events of the last few years in which she and Jem were involved as they must have been seen by Boo Radley, watching the children he loved. She is 'standing in his shoes'. Scout joins Atticus, who is sitting in Jem's room, reading one of Jem's books. He reads aloud to her until she falls asleep. She has learned that most people are 'real nice' when you finally see them.

raling Sounding as if coming from a diseased lung.

Seckatary Hawkins See note on *The Grey Ghost*, p.25.

Revision questions on Part 2

1 Write an account of Jem and Scout's visit with Calpurnia to the Negro church service.

2 Indicate the advantages and disadvantages, from Scout's point of view, of her aunt's coming to stay in Maycomb.

3 Show how Jem, Scout and Dill continue to think about Boo Radley throughout Part 2 of the novel.

4 Write an account of the part played in the story by Mr Underwood, editor of the *Maycomb Tribune*.

5 Narrate the events of the Sunday evening when there is an attempt to break into Maycomb jail.

6 Describe the home life of the Ewells.

7 Explain the main points which Atticus establishes in his questioning of Bob and Mayella Ewell and Tom Robinson, and summarize Atticus's speech to the jury.

8 Describe the different reactions to the jury's verdict of each of the following: (*a*) Jem; (*b*) Miss Stephanie Crawford; (*c*) Dill; (*d*) Miss Maudie Atkinson.

9 Write an account of the Missionary Circle tea-party at which Scout helps. What does she learn from it?

10 Describe the Current Events period during which Cecil Jacobs talks of Hitler. Why do Miss Gates's views puzzle Scout?

11 Give an account of the practical joke played upon the Misses Barber.

12 Write an account of the events of the evening of Mrs Merriweather's pageant *as they would have appeared to Arthur (Boo) Radley*, and make clear his part in those events.

The characters

Atticus

As a young man Atticus broke with family tradition, left the homestead at Finch's Landing and went to Montgomery to study law. At the time of the events related in the novel he is nearly fifty years old. He is thus a figure of maturity and reason, with an individuality of outlook and action. Yet he has great affection and loyalty. At the beginning of his career he practised economy and invested his earnings in his brother's education as a doctor. Atticus's wife had died after only seven years of marriage, leaving a son aged six and a daughter aged two, whom he has brought up with the aid of a Black housekeeper. The standards and values Atticus adopts in their upbringing are not always approved by his more conventional sister, but they are completely consistent with his high ideals and actions as a citizen. These ideals are based on his belief in truth, reason, justice and a respect for individual human personality.

'There are some men in this world,' Miss Maudie Atkinson tells Jem, 'who were born to do our unpleasant jobs for us. Your father's one of them.' On another occasion Jem tries to explain how Atticus 'spends his time doin' things that wouldn't get done if nobody did 'em'. That is why Atticus takes on the defence of Tom Robinson: if he didn't, he says, he would never be able to hold up his head in town or to tell his children what to do. 'Before I can live with other folks,' he explains, 'I've got to live with myself. The one thing that doesn't abide by majority rule is a person's conscience.' Atticus realizes that Tom Robinson has no chance of acquittal but he takes on the case in order to champion truth and justice. He is sorry for Mayella Ewell, but he is not for 'preserving polite fiction' at the expense of human life; and he acts on his beliefs, even at the risk of his personal safety. In court Atticus exposes Ewell's perjury and relentlessly, but courteously, cross-examines Mayella; but it gives him no pleasure to do so. He never separates the law from the human beings who must administer it; 'A court is only as sound as its jury, and a jury is only as sound as the men who make it up', and he has no wish to exempt even his own son from the law when, for a short time, he thinks that Jem killed Bob Ewell.

Atticus never fails to consider the human situation of his clients; if, like Mr Cunningham, they are poor, he accepts payment in kind; and, as a result, they respect him greatly. Even though he fails to gain an acquittal for Tom Robinson, the Blacks in the Coloured balcony stand when Atticus leaves the courtroom, and the Reverend Sykes says they have no better friend. For Atticus makes no distinction of colour or background. Scout reports him as saying that God 'is loving folks like you love yourself', and the great lesson he teaches his children is that of compassion.

Atticus seems able to effect a natural and sympathetic understanding with all those with whom he comes into contact. He talks with young Walter Cunningham about farming as though he were an adult; he knows the ways of country folk; and he knows better than to fuss over the shy Boo Radley when he is received in the Finch home at the end of the book. Atticus considers the personal insults he sometimes receives because he is defending Tom Robinson as an indication of the poverty of spirit of those who hurl them. He understands the reason for Mrs Dubose's viciousness and regards her as 'the bravest person I ever knew'; and when Bob Ewell spits in his face, Atticus merely says he wishes Ewell wouldn't chew tobacco. In fact, he misjudges how far Ewell is prepared to go – his goodness and his faith in reason simply prevent him from imagining the worst.

Atticus's relations with his children are somewhat out of the ordinary. He treats them with 'courteous detachment'. He is rational and realistic. He answers all their questions, explaining everything from entailment to rape, exactly and unemotionally, without 'making a production of it' – for he knows that children can quickly spot an evasion. Atticus is 'the same in his house as he is on the public streets'. He is scupulously fair and always hears both sides of his children's disputes, accepting new situations with humour and good sense, without dogmatism or prejudice. He never chastises his children (and they respect him greatly for that) and he forbids them to fight; his advice is, 'Try fighting with your head for a change'. Atticus's pride in them is often slyly expressed but he defends them against Aunt Alexandra's criticisms. He takes pleasure in puncturing his sister's family pretensions and is uncomfortable when he has to play the role of the conventional father. But Atticus is greatly concerned for them and for what they will have to put up with as a result of his defence of Tom Robinson. However, he does not believe his children should be *too* sheltered – the trial and the issues behind it are 'just as much Maycomb County as missionary teas' – and he hopes that they will not catch 'Maycomb's usual disease', that is, anti-Black prejudice.

They are disappointed that he is not more active physically, and does not enjoy playing strenuous games like the fathers of their friends. However, Miss Maudie Atkinson shows how they have the benefit of their father's age, and the mad dog episode does much to alter their opinion, especially when they understand his reticence about his reputation as One-Shot Finch. He has a withering sense of humour (consider, for example, some of his remarks about Mr Underwood) and he is sometimes quite impertinent (as in his retort to his sister's talk about family 'streaks' in Chapter 13). Atticus always knows more than the children suspect and he is not above trapping them with his 'lawyer's tricks'.

His warm understanding does not prevent him from treating his children with great firmness and he demands from them the strictest obedience to Calpurnia and Aunt Alexandra.

At the end Atticus has helped them to learn an important lesson: most people are 'real nice' when you finally see and understand them.

Scout

Everything in the novel is seen through Scout's eyes, and this includes her own character.

At the beginning of the story, Scout (Jean Louise) Finch is almost six. She is intelligent, lively and precocious. Though her personal experience is naturally limited (for instance she has never seen snow until the winter when Miss Maudie's house burns down), her imagination has been developed and strengthened by her reading – and she could read long before she went to school. Scout is a perspicacious observer, though of course she does not always realize at the time the full significance of what she sees and reports. Above all, she is unprejudiced – she has the ingenuousness of childhood. At the same time she is a realistic character. Scout can be unreasonable and impertinent; she is unhappy at school (and even tries to catch ringworm in the hope that she will have to stay at home); she is a tomboy, 'usually mud-splashed or covered with sand', with a childish romantic love for Dill.

Scout has a very close relationship with her father, for she can remember nothing of her mother, and she feels great loyalty towards him. When Cecil Jacobs announces that Atticus 'defends niggers', her immediate reaction is to pick a fight with him; the next day, after her father has had a talk with her, she takes a different view of the situation: 'Atticus so rarely asked Jem and me to do something for him, I could take being called a coward for him.' When her cousin Francis angers her, she punches him; but she does not wish Atticus to know that it was because Francis had been criticizing him.

Scout maintains her childish dignity – in face of Aunt Alexandra, Uncle Jack and Jem. She does not always understand Jem; she sometimes finds his maddening superiority unbearable; and she is aware of when, because of the difference in their ages, they 'first began to part company' (Chapter 6). Later, Dill's unhappiness at home makes her realize how lucky she is.

Scout has an unselfconscious friendliness and a natural courtesy in her wish to talk to people about what *they* are interested in; on the occasion of the attack planned by the Cunninghams on Maycomb jail, her interest in the human problems of her neighbours probably saves her father's life. Later, this same quality brings her up against the conventional barriers of class and what is and is not accepted in the polite social world of Maycomb.

At times Scout feels that she gets on better with men than with women, whose motives seem to her less open. However, in helping at the Missionary Circle tea-party and learning much from her aunt and Miss Maudie, she begins to appreciate what is involved in being 'a lady'. About this time she also begins to feel remorse 'at·ever having taken part in what must have been sheer torment to Arthur Radley'.

Scout continues to worry about the inconsistencies of adults, finding it hard to reconcile Miss Gates's lesson on Hitler and the Jews with her teacher's opinions on Blacks. But again she learns much when she stands on the Radley porch and sees all that has happened from Boo Radley's point of view. Once again she has learned her father's lesson by standing in someone's shoes.

'Jem and I would get grown up,' says Scout, with the confidence of childhood, 'but there wasn't much else left for us to learn, except possibly algebra.' In fact she understands the final events of the story more quickly than Atticus himself does, for the full significance of Boo Radley's part in them has to be explained to him by the sheriff.

Jem

As Scout narrates her brother's part in, and his reaction to, the events of the story we not only see the way in which he matures; we are able to trace his growing sensitivity and his insight into aspects of the adult world (the truth about Boo Radley, the colour problem, and so on). Scout notes the signs she observes in him: she does not always know what they are signs *of*, and so to her his behaviour is sometimes inexplicable.

Jem (Jeremy Atticus Finch) is nearly ten when the story begins and at first he is completely absorbed in boyish activities – his games, the tree house, acting out the boys' stories which he reads. He is 'football crazy' and has superstitious ideas about things like Hot Steams. He is a very conscious of being four years older than Scout; at times he taunts her for being a girl and yet (when it is convenient for him) he is filled with a sense of responsibility for his 'little sister'. He accepts school more easily than Scout, assuring her that later on she will find it more congenial.

Jem's ambition is to become a lawyer, like his father, and towards the end of the story he is already beginning to have long discussions with Atticus on legal points. Sometimes Jem is disappointed that Atticus never engages in spectacular physical activity, as the fathers of his schoolmates do, but after Atticus shoots the mad dog he becomes a hero in the eyes of his son, who even begins to understand why one doesn't boast of such things. 'Atticus is a gentleman,' he says, 'just like me!'

We see Jem's growing confidence; he walks past Mrs Dubose's house without fear and, learning from his talks with Atticus, he tries to 'hold his head high and be a gentleman'. Scout finds it difficult to understand this 'phase of self-conscious rectitude'. We know that he is gradually gaining greater insight into the world around him. He almost realizes the truth about Boo Radley's situation and is unhappy and even (as on the night of the fire) quite disturbed about it.

Jem has 'a naturally tranquil disposition' and yet he suddenly goes wild and destroys Mrs Dubose's camellias. This is perhaps part of the strain of adolescence which he is experiencing about this time. He no longer wishes to be accompanied in public by his younger sister and when his sense of responsibility extends to his informing Atticus of Dill's clandestine reappearance, Scout considers he has treacherously broken their childhood code. Jem has his father's determination, as seen in his defiance of Atticus's order to leave the Maycomb jail and to go home. At the same time, he shows an affectionate understanding of Scout's anxieties. Jem is beginning to adopt an adult viewpoint and the adults are beginning to acknowledge this: Calpurnia calls him 'Mister Jem' and, while Scout and Dill have little cakes, for Jem Miss Maudie cuts a slice from the big cake. He has an adult (though purely academic) discussion on rape with the Reverend Sykes, saying that Scout is too young to know what they are talking about; and yet a few moments later, he is weeping with disappointment at the verdict. He is so upset that, even some time later, he cannot bear to have the court-house mentioned; he cannot yet see the law objectively, as later he will have to learn to do if he is to become a lawyer.

Just as he has his father's determination, Jem also begins to develop his tact. When Scout muffs her part in the pageant he is so tactful that she says, 'Jem was becoming almost as good as Atticus at making you feel right when things went wrong.' On this important evening the greatest challenge for him as knight-errant comes when he and Scout are attacked by Bob Ewell.

Dill

Charles Baker Harris, who spends his summer in Maycomb with his aunt, Miss Rachel Haverford, is small, precocious and of strange appearance, with snow-white hair and blue linen shorts that button to his shirt. Dill's most important characteristic is his vivid imagination, which feeds on the ideas he has gained from the books he reads. These he turns into plays, which he and Scout and Jem act out endlessly and in which Dill, 'a villain's villain', could get into any character part assigned to him. He makes up romantic stories of fantastic adventures on his journeys each summer from Meridian to Maycomb. Scout describes him as 'a pocket Merlin, whose head teemed with eccentric plans, strange longings, and quaint fancies'; and it is Dill who dares Jem to go to the Radley Place and invents the game of 'making Boo Radley come out'. His quick thinking about strip poker saves Jem from an awkward situation; he regards Scout as his girl and has some naïve ideas about marriage and babies. 'Beautiful things floated around in his dreamy head.'

Miss Harper Lee presents Dill's home life as a contrast with that of Jem and Scout. His parents have separated; he sees little of his father, and his mother packs him off to his aunt every summer. When she remarries, Dill is at first proud of his new stepfather and they plan to build a boat together; but it is soon clear that the situation has never really changed. His parents buy him everything he wants – on condition that he never troubles *them*; they are simply not interested in him and not prepared to give him either attention or affection. It is not surprising that this, coupled with his observation of the treatment which Tom Robinson receives, leads him to become completely disillusioned with adults. Almost cynically he says he will be a clown: 'There ain't one thing in this world I can do about folks except laugh.'

Aunt Alexandra and other relatives

Aunt Alexandra is Atticus's younger sister, who remained at the family homestead, Finch's Landing, and married James Hancock ('Uncle Jimmy'), 'a taciturn man who spent most of his time lying in a hammock by the river wondering if his trot-lines were full' and one for whom Scout had very little regard. Their son, Henry, had left home 'as soon as was humanly possible' and *his* son was Francis, who spent every Christmas with his grandparents while his parents 'pursued their own pleasures'.

At one time Scout used to think that Aunt Alexandra had more in common with Miss Stephanie Crawford than with the other Finches. She is a forceful character with no self-doubt, who manages the lives of all those around her; she arranges, advises, cautions and warns and has a way of declaring 'What Is Best For The Family'. She is particularly fanatical on the subject of Scout's attire and she has a preoccupation with heredity, 'pointing out the shortcomings of other tribal groups to the greater glory of her own'. Scout's only compensation for having to spend Christmas at Finch's Landing (in close contact with Francis) is that her aunt is a good cook. When Aunt Alexandra comes to stay in Maycomb, to provide some feminine influence, she forbids the children to visit Calpurnia at her home or to ask young Walter Cunningham home to dinner. Her ideas on bringing up children almost exactly oppose those of Atticus. But their aunt has a sense of propriety and at a time of crisis (on the day of the Missionary Circle tea-party) she displays great strength of character; she also reveals her anxiety and concern for her brother, whom she sees as being torn to pieces by the demands which are being made on him. In the end, Scout comes to see Aunt Alexandra as a warm and understanding human being.

Jack Finch is ten years younger than Atticus, who has helped to pay for his training as a doctor. He has a sense of humour, teases Miss Maudie and keeps the children laughing. But he doesn't really understand children, evading their questions and failing to respect their sense of fair play by not hearing both sides of a dispute. In this respect Jack provides a contrast with Atticus, who even reads him a lecture on these matters.

Scout's cousin Francis is a despicable child. He taunts Scout, tells tales and insults Atticus. Scout says, 'He enjoyed everything I disapproved of, and disliked my ingenious diversions.'

In Chapter 9 there is a brief description of another member of the Finch family. This is Cousin Ike Finch, Maycomb County's sole surviving Confederate veteran.

Miss Maudie Atkinson

Of all the characters in *To Kill a Mockingbird*, Miss Maudie Atkinson is the one who is most like Atticus, and she has something of the same function. She stands for calm reason and human understanding, and is opposed to any form of prejudice and bigotry – the prejudice of Maycomb's anti-Black feeling or the bigotry of a fundamentalist religious sect. Like Atticus, she treats the children as adults, as rational human beings.

Miss Maudie's personality is individual almost to the point of eccentricity. She keeps a cow, works in her garden in an old straw hat and a man's boiler suit, and amuses the children with a trick with her dentures. She is a benign presence, generous and friendly; she allows the children to play on her lawn and whenever she bakes – she makes the best cakes in the neighbourhood – she bakes three small cakes specially for Jem, Scout and Dill.

Miss Maudie hates her house and spends all her time in her

garden, for she loves anything that grows. Ironically, the fire that burned down her house was probably caused by her love of plants, for one cold night she kept a fire in her kitchen for her potted plants. But she views the catastrophe with philosophic fortitude, 'Always wanted a smaller house.'

She has an acid tongue – 'when Miss Maudie was angry her brevity was icy' – but she is enlightened and sympathetic.

She never told on us, had never played cat-and-mouse with us, she was not at all interested in our private lives. She was our friend. (Chapter 5, p.50)

In evening talks with Scout on her porch, Miss Maudie often explains the real significance of Atticus's remarks and actions. She stoutly defies the critical remarks of foot-washing Baptists and refuses to join in the excitement that surrounds the trial of Tom Robinson – she despises the townspeople for making some-one's misfortune into 'a Roman carnival', a matter of spectacle and emotion. When the trial is over she understands just how low the children are feeling – she gives them cake, wise counsel and sympathetic encouragement: 'We're making a step – it's just a baby-step, but it's a step.'

Her quietly scathing remarks puncture the pretentious hypo-crisy of the ladies of the Missionary Circle. These, and her support of Aunt Alexandra in time of need, show Scout what is really involved in being 'a lady'. Miss Maudie movingly expresses her humble admiration of Atticus: 'We're paying the highest tribute we can pay to a man. We trust him to do right.'

Other ladies of Maycomb

Scout is more at ease with men than with many of the ladies who are her neighbours. Eventually she realizes that she 'must soon enter this world, where on its surface fragrant ladies rocked slowly, fanned gently, and drank cool water'.

Miss Stephanie Crawford

While the two children realize that no one with a grain of sense trusted Miss Stephanie Crawford, she is their main source of information for their melodramatic notions of Boo Radley. Miss Crawford has the reputation of going about doing good but in reality she is 'a neighbourhood scold' who feeds on dramatic happenings, an 'English Channel of gossip', her nose quivering with curiosity for the latest piece of scandal. The trial of Tom Robinson and the threats of Bob Ewell make her tremble with excitement. She plays down the danger from Harry Johnson's mad dog and teases Scout unpleasantly at the Missionary Circle tea-party.

Mrs Henry Lafayette Dubose

The children are almost as scared of Mrs Dubose as they are of Boo Radley. She is old and fearsome; Scout describes her as 'vicious'; and it is rumoured that she keeps a pistol in her shawl. She loudly voices her opinion about Atticus's way of bringing up children and his 'lawing for niggers' and says he is 'no better than the niggers and the trash he works for'. Eventually the children understand the reason for all this – Mrs Dubose is a very sick woman whose medical treatment has left her addicted to morphine, an addiction she is determined to break before she dies. Jem's reading sessions help her to do this and when she dies Atticus helps them to appreciate her courage. 'She died beholden to nothing and to nobody,' he explains. 'She was the bravest person I ever knew.'

Mrs Grace Merriweather

This faithful Methodist, who 'played her voice like an organ', is a member of the Missionary Circle. She is much concerned about the squalid lives of the distant Mrunas, having been greatly impressed by the talk of the saintly J. Grimes Everett; but she patronizingly ignores the problems of Helen Robinson, 'If we just let them know we forgive 'em, that we've forgotten it, then this whole thing'll blow over.' Mrs Merriweather writes and produces the Halloween pageant, in which the schoolchildren are oddly costumed to represent the county's agricultural products.

Mrs Gertrude Farrow

Another member of the Missionary Circle and 'the second most devout lady in Maycomb'. She is 'a splendidly built woman with pale eyes and narrow feet' and everything she says is prefaced by a soft sibilant sound. Mrs Farrow believes that no lady in Maycomb is safe from assault by Blacks.

The Misses Barber
Sarah and Frances Barber are known as Miss Tutti and Miss Frutti. They are both deaf and Miss Frutti has an enormous ear trumpet. Maycomb considers their ways are strange, especially as they have a cellar dug beneath their house. As a Halloween prank 'some wicked children' stealthily remove all their furniture and hide it in the cellar, where it is only discovered after Mr Heck Tate has put hounds on the trail.

Miss Rachel Haverford
Miss Haverford is Dill's aunt, with whom he stays during his summer holidays. She is fierce and strict and given to explosive utterances like 'Do-oo Je-sus'; but underneath she has a kind nature.

We also meet two of Scout's schoolteachers – Miss Caroline Fisher, a new teacher who 'looked and smelled like a peppermint drop' and has almost as much to learn as her pupils (Chapters 2 and 3); and Miss Gates, whose opinions on Hitler's treatment of the Jews are inconsistent with her comments on Maycomb's treatment of Tom Robinson (Chapter 26).

The Cunninghams

The Cunninghams are described as 'an enormous and confusing tribe ... The nearest thing to a gang ever seen in Maycomb'. They have a history of coming up against the law; Boo Radley joined one group of tearaways whose high-spirited exploits led to their being sent to an industrial school and his being isolated at home. One of the Cunningham disputes over land titles furnished the only occasion on which Judge Taylor had been stumped on a legal point (Chapter 16). The Cunninghams pride themselves on their independence. 'They never took anything off of anybody, they get along with what they have,' Scout tells Miss Fisher, and Atticus explains that once you earned their respect they were for you tooth and nail. The Cunninghams are farmers and have been hit hard by the economic crisis. They are so poor that when Walter Cunningham consults Atticus on a legal matter, in connection with the entailment of his land, he has to pay in kind, with nuts and vegetables. His son, young Walter, takes no lunch to school and on the day when he has lunch with the Finches he pours syrup on his vegetables, much to Scout's horror. But she soon learns that, though he lacks education and social graces, Walter is basically sound: he knows more about life than Scout and Jem and can discuss adult matters in an adult way. 'That Walter's as smart as can be, he just gets held back sometimes because he has to stay out and help his daddy.'

Later Walter's father, carried away by the feelings which are running high in Maycomb, joins the mob which is preparing to attack Atticus and lynch Tom Robinson – until Scout's intervention pulls him up short and makes him aware of his position as a man and as a father.

Finally, it is another Cunningham who is responsible for the time taken by the jury in reaching its verdict – a small but important step forward in the fight against prejudice.

The Ewells

Living in their sordid cabin behind the town garbage dump, the Ewells have been the disgrace of Maycomb for three generations. They are idle spongers, living on national relief. 'They were people, but they lived like animals.' In his cross-examination of Mayella, Atticus elicits a picture of the sordid home-life of the dirty and illiterate Ewell children.

Burris Ewell, whose lice horrify Miss Fisher, is the filthiest human being Scout has ever seen. Like his father, he is belligerent and insolent.

Mayella, 'a thick-bodied girl accustomed to strenuous labour', is ignorant and furtive, always on the defensive and ready to disguise her fear in insolence. She is 'the victim of cruel poverty and ignorance' and lives in fear of her father. Yet 'she seemed to try more'n the rest of 'em'; she is sensitive to beauty and tends with care a row of red geraniums. She feels the need for kindness and affection, and at one point Scout realizes 'that Mayella Ewell must have been the loneliest person in the world. She was even lonelier than Boo Radley'. Tom Robinson was probably the only person who was ever decent to her. Her unforgiveable mistake is that in seeking the affection of a Black she breaks 'a rigid and time-honoured code of our society' and then, like a child, tries to destroy the evidence of her guilt.

Most of the real responsibility lies upon the father, Bob Ewell, who has no concern or affection for Mayella. He beats his children and spends his charity allowance on drink. He is ignorant, insolent and quarrelsome, and filled with passionate enmity. His crude language causes disorder in the courtroom. After the trial, because he has been proved a liar and because it is clear that it was he who had given Mayella her bruises, his animosity smoulders: he tries to burgle Judge Taylor's house, molests Helen Robinson and spits in Atticus's face, threatening that he will 'get him'. Finally Bob Ewell attacks Jem and Scout as they are returning from the Halloween pageant and is killed by their rescuer, Arthur Radley.

The Radleys

Early in the story we are given a description of the Radley Place, a house of mystery and misery, untidy and neglected in an overgrown garden. Both the house and its occupants have become associated with fear and suspicion in the imaginations of most people in Maycomb, and certainly in the imaginations of Jem, Scout and Dill, fed by their sensational childhood reading.

The Radleys are unfriendly people, foot-washing Baptists with strict and narrow ideas. Old Mr Radley, 'a thin leathery man with colourless eyes', is described by Calpurnia as 'the meanest man God ever blew breath into'. He goes to work every day but has few contacts with his neighbours since his younger son Arthur had come up against the law some twenty years previously. Promising that his son would cause no further trouble, Mr Radley had kept him shut up inside the house. 'From the day Mr Radley took Arthur home, people said the house died', and not surprisingly strange stories grew, like the one that alleged that Arthur had made a homicidal attack on his father with a pair of scissors.

When Mr Radley dies, his elder son, Nathan, comes back from Pensacola to look after the place. Though he occasionally speaks to the neighbours, he is in reality no more friendly than his father had been. When Jem trespasses in his garden one evening he fires his shotgun, and after Jem has delivered a thank-you note for the presents in the tree Mr Radley stops up the knothole with cement.

The nature of the story demands that Boo Radley (Arthur) remains throughout a mysterious and shadowy figure. In the children's imagination he has grown into an almost super-

humanly terrifying figure; nevertheless, they want to see him –
and on two occasions they very nearly do. The reader comes to
see Boo Radley in a much less melodramatic light – a pathetic
recluse who regards the children from a distance with affection.
For him they represent the children he has never had. He leaves
gifts for them in the knot-hole of a tree (Chapters 4 and 7);
watching from inside the house, he shares in and laughs at the
amusement of their games (Chapter 4); he roughly mends the
tear in Jem's trousers and folds them neatly to await his return;
he puts a blanket round Scout's shoulders as she stands
shivering on the pavement, watching Miss Maudie Atkinson's
house burn down. Eventually Scout and Jem come to see him as
a sad figure and are almost ashamed of their earlier games. We
learn no more of Boo Radley's actions until he saves the children's lives by killing Bob Ewell and carries Jem gently home.
When Scout sees him standing unobtrusively in Jem's bedroom
she does not at first recognize him – 'He was some countryman I
did not know.' He is pale and fearful: he gives Scout a timid
smile and lightly touches the sleeping Jem in affection. We
realize how Scout's 'small fantasy' of meeting 'Mr Arthur' as she
might meet any other neighbour (Chapter 26) has at last come
true when she accompanies him back to his home.

Other citizens of Maycomb

Mr Heck Tate
In his high boots, lumber jacket and bullet-studded belt, the
sheriff of Maycomb County is at first something of a terrifying
figure to Scout. He investigated the burglary at the Misses Barber; he accompanies Atticus when the latter shoots Harry
Johnson's mad dog; the sheriff is one of the group who come to
the Finch house late one Saturday evening, fearing trouble at
the jail. However, when he testifies at Tom Robinson's trial he
wears an ordinary business suit and from that moment he ceases
to terrify Scout. Heck Tate is a solid and reliable upholder of the
law, slow and deliberate of speech but firm and enlightened in
his method. Ewell's attack on the children was not such a surprise to him as it was to Atticus, for Sheriff Tate judges men by
different standards; but he is determined that Boo Radley shall
never be brought to trial for having to kill Ewell and he will insist
that what happened was that Ewell fell on his own knife.

Judge Taylor

Amiable and white-haired, looking in court 'like a sleepy old shark', Judge Taylor is another very human officer of the law. Atticus regards him as a very good judge and certainly he was wise in naming Atticus to defend Tom Robinson. Only once was he ever known to be exasperated – and that was by a case involving Cunninghams (Chapter 16). Though he runs his court with informality, chewing an unlighted cigar throughout the proceedings, he runs it with a firm grip, standing no nonsense from either witnesses or attorneys.

Mr Underwood

Mr Braxton Bragg Underwood is the owner, editor and printer of the town's newspaper: 'It was said that he made up every edition of the *Maycomb Tribune* out of his own head and wrote it down on the linotype.' He appears to watch everything – he knows, for instance, that the children had been in the Coloured balcony of the courtroom 'since precisely one-eighteen p.m.'. 'An intense profane little man', he has usually no time for organized social action; but the Tom Robinson affair is serious enough to make him join Atticus and others. Mr Underwood despises Blacks but believes passionately in justice; and so he keeps Atticus covered with his shotgun during the attempt on the jail and writes a humane editorial on the shooting of Tom Robinson.

Dr Reynolds

Brisk, joking and friendly, Dr Reynolds had brought Jem and Scout into the world, led them through their childhood diseases and never lost their friendship. He is another member of that group of professional men who show concern for Atticus's safety on the weekend of the attack on the jail.

Mr Dolphus Raymond

This strange but likeable character lives with a Black woman 'and all sorts of mixed children' (gossip has it that because of her, his white fiancée killed herself after the wedding rehearsal). The whole of Maycomb believes that Mr Dolphus Raymond lurches through life half-drunk on whisky, which he drinks from a Coca-Cola bottle in a bag. He is therefore labelled 'an evil man'. Only Jem, Scout and Dill know the truth and in learning from him his secret they learn much else besides. Mr Raymond is a man of great kindness, much upset by 'the simple hell people give other people' and, since the people of Maycomb could never understand why he lives as he does, he gives them a reason for their disapproval by *pretending* to be a drunkard.

Mr Link Deas
This is another character who strengthens the children's faith in adult human nature. Mr Deas is a very considerate employer of Tom and Helen Robinson. He interrupts the court proceedings by defending Tom's character, looks after Helen after Tom's death, and quickly puts a stop to Ewell's pestering of her.

Mr Avery
One of the Finches' neighbours, Mr Avery is something of an eccentric. He is continually sneezing and has some very odd ideas about the inscriptions on the Rosetta stone. The children are astonished and impressed by his feat of urination one evening and their snowman is made to resemble him. Though Mr Avery is linked with Miss Stephanie Crawford as a gossip, he works very hard, and at considerable personal risk, in helping to save Miss Maudie Atkinson's furniture when her house burns down.

Other characters who appear, or are referred to, briefly are: Mr Gilmer, the solicitor from Abbotsville (Chapters 17 and 18), Sam Levy (Chapter 15) and Mr X Billups (Chapter 16).

The Blacks

Calpurnia
Atticus's cook and housekeeper is a substitute mother, who shares with Atticus the task of bringing up his children, an undertaking in which she succeeds admirably. She is 'a faithful member of his family' and Atticus could not have got along without her. In defending her against his sister's criticisms, Atticus says:

I don't think the children've suffered one bit from her having brought them up. If anything she's been harder on them in some ways than a mother would have been ... she's never let them get away with anything, she's never indulged them in the way most coloured nurses do. She's tried to bring them up according to her lights, and Cal's lights are pretty good – and another thing, the children love her. (Chapter 14, p.140)

At first Scout talks of 'her tyrannical presence' and is conscious of her hand being 'as wide as a bed slat and twice as hard'; and it is true that Calpurnia is without sentimentality and can, on occasion, be quite fierce. But in everything she is motivated by her real love for the children. Calpurnia was taught her letters by Miss Maudie's aunt and learned to read by working through Atticus's law books. She in turn taught Scout to write – and much else besides, including the proper way to treat one's 'company'. In the mad-dog episode she shows firmness and courage. On their visit to her church, the children are struck by the fact that she has one way of talking with white people and another when she is with her own people. They learn much from her 'modest double life' and her simple wisdom in accepting that you cannot change people if they do not want to change themselves. Calpurnia has come to accept and live with the differences between Black and White.

Tom Robinson

Tom is a gentle character, 'a quiet, respectable, humble Negro', who is employed by Mr Link Deas in cotton picking and general work. His left arm is useless, having been injured in a cotton gin. Tom is a thoughtful and respectful person: when asked to say what Ewell had called him he does not think it fitting that the children in the court-house should hear the expression, and it occurs to Scout 'that, in their own way, Tom Robinson's manners were as good as Atticus's'. But his kindness is his undoing – he is sorry for Maybella Ewell because 'Mr Ewell didn't seem to help her none', and her reaction leads to his being charged with rape – the Black *must* be to blame, not the white girl. After the verdict, Tom loses all hope of a successful appeal against it and he is senselessly killed in a blindly instinctive attempt to escape from prison.

Tom's wife, Helen, is another gentle soul, who receives much help from Mr Link Deas.

Reverend Sykes

The Minister of First Purchase Methodist Episcopal Church is a short, stocky man, with infinite charity, the ability to preach a forthright sermon denouncing sin and a firmness in handling his congregation. In the court-house he takes the children under his wing in the Coloured balcony. Like all the Blacks, he feels great respect and gratitude for Atticus.

Zeebo

The garbage collector is Calpurnia's son. She has taught him to read and in church his task as 'music superintendent' is to lead the congregation by 'lining' the hymns.

The only Black who is not sympathetic to the Finch children is Lula, who thinks they should not be visiting First Purchase Church.

General questions plus questions on related topics for coursework/examinations on other books you may be studying.

1 Develop in some detail the contrast between the characters of Miss Maudie Atkinson and Mrs Henry Lafayette Dubose.

Suggested notes for essay answer:

For most of the story the two ladies *seem* to be very different.

(a) Miss Maudie is understanding, balanced in her views, reasonable, unprejudiced. Consider her attitude to the anti-Black feeling in Maycomb and to the fundamentalist religious views of the Mennonites and the foot-washing Baptists.

Mrs Dubose is very prejudiced. Consider her attitude to the Blacks, whom she regards as 'trash'.

(b) Miss Maudie is a friendly person, with a sense of humour (note her teasing of Jack Finch in Chapter 5). She is helpful to Jem, Scout and Dill: she bakes them cakes and lets them play in her garden. Further, she understands their feelings at awkward moments (*e.g.* after the trial and at the Missionary Circle tea-party). She is a 'benign presence'.

Mrs Dubose is old and ill. It is the general opinion that she is 'the meanest old woman who ever lived'. She has no time for the children, who find her very fearsome, for she loudly criticizes them as they pass her house. (Her house is very different from Miss Maudie's, as they find out when Jem has to read to Mrs Dubose.)

(c) Miss Maudie greatly admires Atticus, his way of bringing up his children, his work for the people of Maycomb and his defence of Tom Robinson; and she very much helps in the children's increasing understanding of their father.

Mrs Dubose is outwardly very critical of Atticus – of the way he is bringing up his children and his defence of Tom Robinson ('lawing for niggers') – but inwardly she has a good deal of respect for him and the way he helps her at the end of her life (see Chapter 11).

Yet –

both ladies

(a) are eccentric (Miss Maudie's cow, her boiler suit, her trick with her dentures; Mrs Dubose is thought to keep a pistol in her shawls and wraps).

(b) can express themselves very sharply (Miss Maudie has an acid tongue at times; Scout says Mrs Dubose is 'vicious').

(c) show courage and strength of character in the face of misfortune and adversity – Miss Maudie when her house burns down and Mrs Dubose in her fight against illness and subsequent morphine addiction. (Atticus says, 'She was the bravest person I ever knew.')

2 'When he was nearly thirteen, my brother Jem got his arm badly broken at the elbow.' Explain how this opening sentence is a good starting point for the series of events which form the story of *To Kill a Mockingbird*.

3 'Atticus Finch is the same in his house as he is on the public streets.' Explain what Miss Maudie means by these words and, referring to both his professional and his private life, say what you think are Atticus's most important qualities.

4 'You never really understand a person until you consider things from his point of view – until you climb into his skin and walk around in it,' says Atticus. Choose *two* of the people Jem and Scout learn to understand in the course of the novel and say through what experiences the children 'climb into their skins'.

5 What does the character of Dill contribute to the story and to the ideas and themes of *To Kill a Mockingbird*?

6 Write an account of Scout's experiences in school, both in class and at the Halloween pageant.

7 Write a description of Calpurnia and show her importance in the development of Scout's character.

8 Write an account of the courtroom proceedings at the trial of Tom Robinson.

9 'The whole life of a "tired old town" in Alabama seems to be caught and preserved in the characters of the family's neighbours.' Describe *three* of these neighbours and show how they are good examples of life in 'a tired old town'.

10 From which *three* characters in the novel do you think Jem and Scout learned most? Discuss, with close reference to the events of the story.

11 With reference to particular incidents in the novel, compare and contrast the attitudes towards and the understanding of children shown by Uncle Jack, Aunt Alexandra and Miss Maudie Atkinson.

12 'I wanted you to see what real courage is, instead of getting the idea that courage is a man with a gun.' To what incident does the phrase 'a man with a gun' refer? What other kinds of courage are shown in *To Kill a Mockingbird*?

13 Explain what Atticus meant when he said that the trial of Tom Robinson was 'just as much Maycomb County as missionary teas' and how this reflects the way he has brought up Jem and Scout.

14 In the light of the events and characters of *To Kill a Mockingbird*, what do you think is the significance of the quotation from Charles Lamb which is used as an epigraph to the novel?

15 What is the significance of the title of this novel? Discuss the symbolism of the mockingbird, considering the several references throughout the novel and the characters and situations to which they are related.

16 Explain why, at first, the children believe Boo Radley to be a 'malevolent phantom'. By tracing the part he plays in the story, show how they are mistaken.

17 Describe in some details the qualities of Atticus (i) as a father, (ii) as a neighbour, and (iii) as a lawyer.

18 Show how the relationship between Scout and Jem changes in the course of the novel.

19 What have you learned from *To Kill a Mockingbird* about the colour problem and the treatment of Blacks in the southern states of the USA during the 1930s?

20 What is contributed to the novel as a whole by the appearance in it at various times of members of the Cunningham family?

21 Describe the many parent–child relationships in this novel and discuss the ways in which some of these relationships contrast with others.

22 Describe Mr Dolphus Raymond and his way of life, and show how, though he plays only a small part in the story, his presence has much to contribute to the theme of *To Kill a Mockingbird*.

23 What contrasts can you draw between the Cunninghams and the Ewells?

24 Aunt Alexandra and Atticus hold very different views on the bringing up of children. Discuss in some detail how their views differ.

25 'I can't live one way in town and another way in my home.' Explain what Atticus means by this and show, by reference to incidents in the story, how his belief governs the way he brings up his children.

26 Give an account of any book or play you have read which contains a trial or court scene, and say how important it is to the plot of the book.

27 Write about any book you know well which deals with questions of racial prejudice or intolerance.

28 Compare Atticus with any character in a book you are studying *or* Write about a character of outstanding qualities in your chosen book.

29 Scout tells the story in her own words. Write about any supposedly autobiographical narration in one of your books.

30 Write about a dramatic or funny incident in one of your set books.

31 Indicate the importance of the setting on the action in a book of your choice.

32 Write about a mysterious or eccentric character in your chosen book.

33 Give a picture of family life as it is described in a book you are studying.

34 Show how the author you are studying establishes a particular atmosphere in his or her book.

35 Write about the presentation of childhood in your chosen book.

Brodie's Notes

Edward Albee	**Who's Afraid of Virginia Woolf?**
Jane Austen	**Emma**
Jane Austen	**Mansfield Park**
Jane Austen	**Pride and Prejudice**
Samuel Beckett	**Waiting for Godot**
William Blake	**Songs of Innocence and Experience**
Robert Bolt	**A Man for All Seasons**
Charlotte Brontë	**Jane Eyre**
Emily Brontë	**Wuthering Heights**
Geoffrey Chaucer	**The Franklin's Tale**
Geoffrey Chaucer	**The Knight's Tale**
Geoffrey Chaucer	**The Miller's Tale**
Geoffrey Chaucer	**The Nun's Priest's Tale**
Geoffrey Chaucer	**The Pardoner's Prologue and Tale**
Geoffrey Chaucer	**Prologue to the Canterbury Tales**
Geoffrey Chaucer	**The Wife of Bath's Tale**
Wilkie Collins	**The Woman in White**
William Congreve	**The Way of the World**
Joseph Conrad	**Heart of Darkness**
Charles Dickens	**Great Expectations**
Charles Dickens	**Hard Times**
Charles Dickens	**Oliver Twist**
Charles Dickens	**A Tale of Two Cities**
Gerald Durrell	**My Family and Other Animals**
George Eliot	**The Mill on the Floss**
George Eliot	**Silas Marner**
T. S. Eliot	**Selected Poems**
Henry Fielding	**Tom Jones**
F. Scott Fitzgerald	**The Great Gatsby and Tender is the Night**
E. M. Forster	**Howard's End**
E. M. Forster	**A Passage to India**
John Fowles	**The French Lieutenant's Woman**
Anne Frank	**The Diary of Anne Frank**
Mrs Gaskell	**North and South**
William Golding	**Lord of the Flies**
Graham Greene	**Brighton Rock**
Graham Greene	**The Power and the Glory**
Graham Handley (ed)	**The Metaphysical Poets: John Donne to Henry Vaughan**
Thomas Hardy	**Far From the Madding Crowd**
Thomas Hardy	**The Mayor of Casterbridge**
Thomas Hardy	**The Return of the Native**
Thomas Hardy	**Tess of the d'Urbervilles**
L. P. Hartley	**The Go-Between**
Aldous Huxley	**Brave New World**
Ben Jonson	**Volpone**
James Joyce	**A Portrait of the Artist as a Young Man**
John Keats	**Selected Poems and Letters of John Keats**
Philip Larkin	**Selected Poems of Philip Larkin**
D. H. Lawrence	**The Rainbow**
D. H. Lawrence	**Sons and Lovers**
D. H. Lawrence	**Women in Love**

List continued overleaf

Harper Lee	**To Kill a Mockingbird**
Laurie Lee	**Cider with Rosie**
Christopher Marlowe	**Dr Faustus**
Arthur Miller	**The Crucible**
Arthur Miller	**Death of a Salesman**
John Milton	**Paradise Lost, Books I and II**
Robert C. O'Brien	**Z for Zachariah**
Sean O'Casey	**Juno and the Paycock**
George Orwell	**Animal Farm**
George Orwell	**1984**
J. B. Priestley	**An Inspector Calls**
J. D. Salinger	**The Catcher in the Rye**
William Shakespeare	**Antony and Cleopatra**
William Shakespeare	**As You Like It**
William Shakespeare	**Hamlet**
William Shakespeare	**Henry IV Part I**
William Shakespeare	**Henry IV Part II**
William Shakespeare	**Julius Caesar**
William Shakespeare	**King Lear**
William Shakespeare	**Macbeth**
William Shakespeare	**Measure for Measure**
William Shakespeare	**The Merchant of Venice**
William Shakespeare	**A Midsummer Night's Dream**
William Shakespeare	**Much Ado about Nothing**
William Shakespeare	**Othello**
William Shakespeare	**Richard II**
William Shakespeare	**Richard III**
William Shakespeare	**Romeo and Juliet**
William Shakespeare	**The Tempest**
William Shakespeare	**Twelfth Night**
George Bernard Shaw	**Arms and the Man**
George Bernard Shaw	**Pygmalion**
Alan Sillitoe	**Selected Fiction**
John Steinbeck	**Of Mice and Men** and **The Pearl**
Jonathan Swift	**Gulliver's Travels**
J. M. Synge	**The Playboy of the Western World**
Dylan Thomas	**Under Milk Wood**
Alice Walker	**The Color Purple**
Virginia Woolf	**To the Lighthouse**
W. B. Yeats	**Selected Poetry**

ENGLISH COURSEWORK BOOKS

Terri Apter	**Women and Society**
Kevin Dowling	**Drama and Poetry**
Philip Gooden	**Conflict**
Philip Gooden	**Science Fiction**
Margaret K. Gray	**Modern Drama**
Graham Handley	**Modern Poetry**
Graham Handley	**Prose**
Graham Handley	**Childhood and Adolescence**
R. J. Sims	**The Short Story**